Eyewitness
FOSSIL

Pleistocene human skull

Eocene gastropods

Eocene fish

Cretaceous dinosaur
finger bones

Triassic swimming reptile

Jurassic brittlestar

Cretaceous
cone (sectioned
and polished)

Cretaceous cone

Ordovician nautiloid
(polished and shaped)

Jurassic sea-urchin

Carboniferous
horsetail

Modern
horsetail

Eocene
shark
tooth

Pleistocene coral

Carboniferous
fern

Jurassic ammonite
(carved as a
snakestone)

Eyewitness
FOSSIL

Triassic
dinosaur
footprint

Written by
DR PAUL D. TAYLOR

In association with
THE NATURAL HISTORY
MUSEUM, LONDON

Carboniferous
lycopod

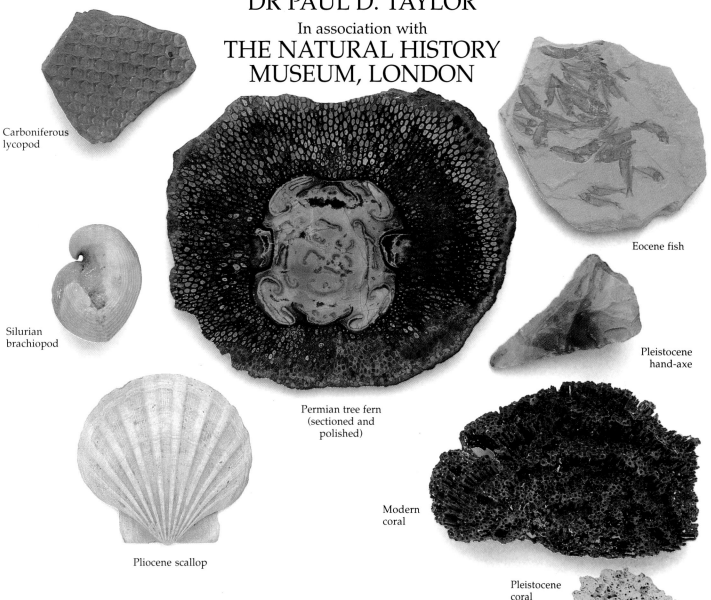

Eocene fish

Silurian
brachiopod

Pleistocene
hand-axe

Permian tree fern
(sectioned and
polished)

Modern
coral

Pliocene scallop

Pleistocene
coral

A Dorling Kindersley Book

Cretaceous
dinosaur tooth

Jurassic
ammonite

Carboniferous spider

Pleistocene sea urchin

Cretaceous
opalized
gastropod

Cretaceous
opalized bivalve

Cretaceous worm tube

Cretaceous bryozoan

Jurassic coral (sectioned
and polished)

Miocene corals

Pleistocene
gastropods

DK

LONDON, NEW YORK, TORONTO,
MELBOURNE, MUNICH, and DELHI

Project editor Louise Pritchard
Art editor Alison Anholt-White
Senior editor Sophie Mitchell
Senior art editor Julia Harris
Editorial director Sue Unstead
Art director Anne-Marie Bulat
Special photography Colin Keates
(Natural History Museum, London)

PAPERBACK EDITION
Managing editors Linda Esposito, Andrew Macintyre
Managing art editor Jane Thomas
Category publisher Linda Martin
Art director Simon Webb
Editor and reference compiler Clare Hibbert
Art editor Joanna Pocock
Consultant Kim Bryan
Production Jenny Jacoby
Picture research Celia Dearing
DTP designer Siu Yin Ho
2 4 6 8 10 9 7 5 3

This Eyewitness ® Guide has been conceived by
Dorling Kindersley Limited and Editions Gallimard
Hardback edition first published in Great Britain in 1990.
This edition first published in Great Britain in 2003
by Dorling Kindersley Limited,
80 Strand, London WC2R 0RL

Copyright © 1990, © 2003, Dorling Kindersley Limited, London
Penguin Group

A CIP catalogue record for this book is
available from the British Library.

ISBN 0 7513 6486 X

Colour reproduction by Colourscan, Singapore
Printed in China by Toppan Co. (Shenzhen) Ltd.

See our complete
catalogue at

www.dk.com

19th-century
microscope for
examining thin
sections

Slide of thin section of
Carboniferous bryozoans

Silurian
sea lily

Miocene bat jaws

Modern
magnolia flower

Contents

Jurassic ammonites

Silurian trilobite (mounted as a brooch)

Fossils-true and false

Fossils ARE THE REMAINS or evidence of animals or plants which have been preserved naturally. They range from the skeletons of huge dinosaurs to tiny plants and animals which can only be seen under a microscope. Most fossils are formed from the hard parts of animals and plants such as shells, bones, teeth, or wood. They may be virtually unchanged from the originals, or be mineral replacements. Animals and plants have also been preserved in peat, tar, ice, and amber, the resin of ancient trees. Eggs, footprints, and burrows can be fossilized too. The study of fossils, called palaeontology, shows us that life originated on Earth at least 3,500 million years ago. Since then there has been a succession of animal and plant species. Most are now extinct and only a tiny proportion have survived as fossils. By studying these survivors, we have a fascinating glimpse of ancient life on Earth.

WHAT CAN IT BE?
People have collected fossils for hundreds of years although the true nature of them was a mystery until relatively recently. This illustration appeared in an Italian book published in 1670.

ONLY BONES
The only remains of animals are often just bones because these are the hardest parts. This is the fossilized vertebra from the backbone of an ancient, giant swimming reptile called a plesiosaur (pp. 46–47).

Trilobite cast and mould

TAKING SHAPE
Fossils are often found in two parts. If, after burial, an animal rots away, it leaves a hollow mould. If this is then filled by sediment (p. 9) it may harden to form a cast.

RARE DELICACY
Detailed fossils of plants are rare because they rot away quickly when they die. In this leaf, however, even the delicate veins have been preserved.

PEARLY AMMONITE
Ammonites (pp. 28-29) are now extinct. They had hard shells made of a chalky mineral called aragonite, with a colourful outer layer of mother-of-pearl. This one has been preserved almost in its original state.

Plesiosaur tooth

HARD TOOTH
Teeth are often found as fossils as they are made of hard material.

PRECIOUS WOOD
One kind of fossilization occurs when chemical changes cause a mineral to grow, grain by grain, in place of the original tissues, or material, of the animal or plant. The tissues of this fossilized wood have been replaced by opal.

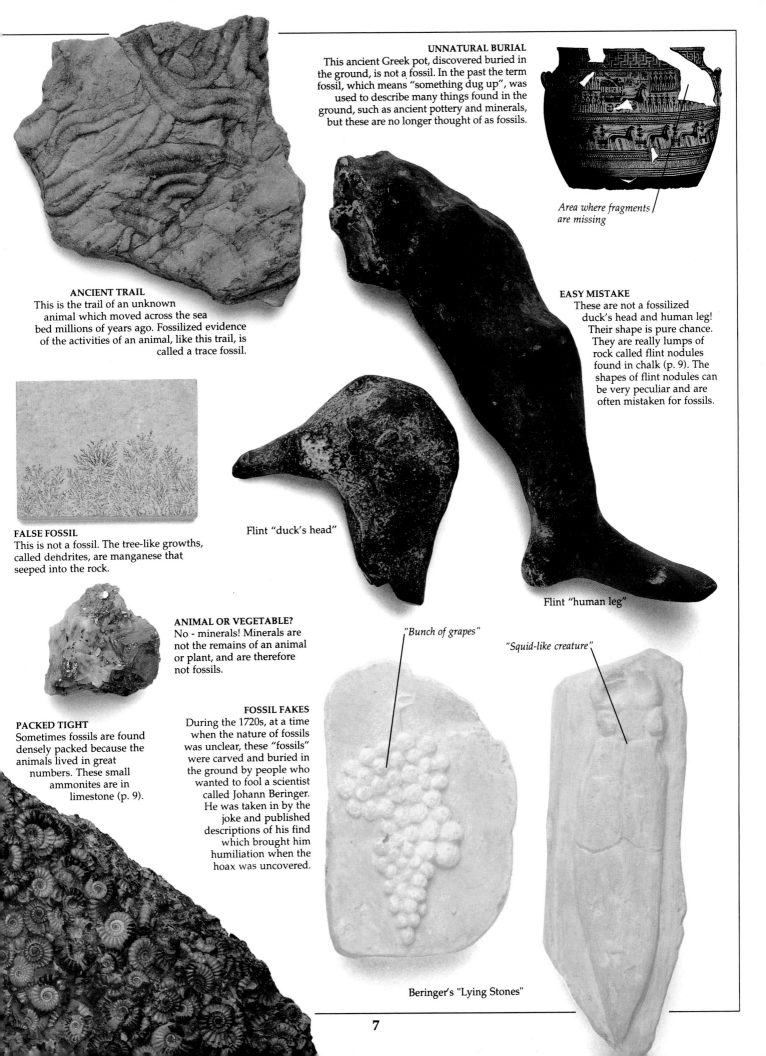

ANCIENT TRAIL
This is the trail of an unknown animal which moved across the sea bed millions of years ago. Fossilized evidence of the activities of an animal, like this trail, is called a trace fossil.

UNNATURAL BURIAL
This ancient Greek pot, discovered buried in the ground, is not a fossil. In the past the term fossil, which means "something dug up", was used to describe many things found in the ground, such as ancient pottery and minerals, but these are no longer thought of as fossils.

Area where fragments are missing

EASY MISTAKE
These are not a fossilized duck's head and human leg! Their shape is pure chance. They are really lumps of rock called flint nodules found in chalk (p. 9). The shapes of flint nodules can be very peculiar and are often mistaken for fossils.

Flint "duck's head"

Flint "human leg"

FALSE FOSSIL
This is not a fossil. The tree-like growths, called dendrites, are manganese that seeped into the rock.

ANIMAL OR VEGETABLE?
No - minerals! Minerals are not the remains of an animal or plant, and are therefore not fossils.

PACKED TIGHT
Sometimes fossils are found densely packed because the animals lived in great numbers. These small ammonites are in limestone (p. 9).

FOSSIL FAKES
During the 1720s, at a time when the nature of fossils was unclear, these "fossils" were carved and buried in the ground by people who wanted to fool a scientist called Johann Beringer. He was taken in by the joke and published descriptions of his find which brought him humiliation when the hoax was uncovered.

"Bunch of grapes"

"Squid-like creature"

Beringer's "Lying Stones"

The making of rocks

AMETHYST
This is the purple variety of the mineral quartz. If allowed to grow freely, quartz crystals are pointed and hexagonal (six-sided).

THE MANY KINDS OF ROCKS beneath our feet have been forming for more than 4,000 million years. The Earth's crust is made up of elements. The important ones are oxygen, silicon, aluminium, iron, calcium, sodium, potassium, magnesium, and carbon. These combine in different ways to form minerals. All rocks are made up of minerals. Common rock-forming minerals include calcite (calcium carbonate), quartz (silicon dioxide), and feldspars (complex minerals containing aluminium, silicon, calcium, sodium, and potassium). There are three groups of rocks: igneous, metamorphic, and sedimentary.

FOLDED ROCK
Powerful movements in the Earth's crust can cause rocks to crack, forming faults, or to buckle, forming folds like this.

Feldspar   *Mica*   *Quartz*

Thin section of granite

Black mica
Glassy quartz
White feldspar

Distorted trilobite

TWISTED TRILOBITE
Metamorphic rocks may contain distorted fossils such as this trilobite (p. 30) in slate.

GRANITE
The speckles in this granite are individual minerals. Granite is an igneous rock formed at great depths.

Molten rocks

Igneous rocks are formed by the cooling of molten magma from deep within the Earth. Sometimes the magma reaches the surface and erupts from volcanoes as lava before it cools. But often, cooling and solidification occur deep underground.

Band rich in mica

Band rich in quartz

Changed rocks

High temperatures and pressures can change rocks into new types called metamorphic rocks. Marble is a metamorphosed limestone, slate a metamorphosed shale.

LAYER UPON LAYER
The Grand Canyon in the U.S.A., formed by the erosion of sandstone and limestone, is a natural slice through the Earth's crust. The oldest stratum, or layer, is at the bottom, the youngest at the top.

SCHIST
Parallel banding of minerals is a common feature of metamorphic rocks. Schist is formed from shale or mud.

Band of quartz
Band of silicate minerals
Thin section of schist

One varve
Fine sediment
Coarse sediment

ROCK BANDS
Stratification on a much smaller scale than the Grand Canyon is seen in this sedimentary rock. Each set of one light layer (fine sediment) and one dark layer (coarse sediment) is a year's accumulation of silt and mud, called a varve, at the bottom of a glacier-fed lake. Such well-defined seasonal bands are rare.

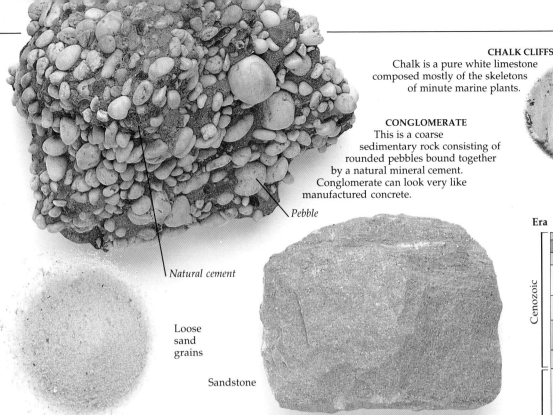

Pebble

Natural cement

CHALK CLIFFS
Chalk is a pure white limestone composed mostly of the skeletons of minute marine plants.

CONGLOMERATE
This is a coarse sedimentary rock consisting of rounded pebbles bound together by a natural mineral cement. Conglomerate can look very like manufactured concrete.

Loose sand grains

Sandstone

Quartz

Iron-rich cement

Thin section of sandstone

Deposited rocks

Rocks are continually being eroded, creating grains which are carried by rivers, by the sea, or by the wind. These grains are deposited, together with the remains of animals and plants, as mud, sand, or coarser material. As this sediment is buried deeper by more sediment, it is compacted, and cemented by the growth of minerals to form a sedimentary rock. Sandstone, for example, is a sedimentary rock made from cemented sand.

FROM ROCK TO ROCK
As cliffs of sedimentary rocks are eroded, small pieces are deposited on the beach. These will be eroded further and may eventually form new sedimentary rock.

Clam shell

FOSSIL CONTAINER
Many sedimentary rocks contain hard lumps called concretions or nodules. These were formed after the sediment was deposited, often around fossil shells like this clam (p. 26).

Shell fragment

Thin section of limestone

Finely broken-up shells

FOSSILIFEROUS ROCK
Limestone is a sedimentary rock composed mainly of calcite and a few other similar carbonate minerals. The calcite is usually derived from the broken-up shells and skeletons of animals and plants which lived in the sea. Larger, more intact shells can also be present, and limestones are therefore good rocks in which to hunt for fossils. This Silurian limestone contains some fossil brachiopods (pp. 24–25).

Fossil brachiopod

Era	Period	Million years ago
Cenozoic	Holocene (Epoch)	0.01
	Pleistocene (Epoch)	2
	Pliocene (Epoch)	5
	Miocene (Epoch)	
		24
	Oligocene (Epoch)	
		34
	Eocene (Epoch)	
		55
	Palaeocene (Epoch)	
		65
Mesozoic	Cretaceous	
		142
	Jurassic	
		206
	Triassic	
		248
Palaeozoic	Permian	
		290
	Carboniferous	
		354
	Devonian	
		417
	Silurian	
		443
	Ordovician	
		495
	Cambrian	
		545
	Precambrian (about seven times longer than all the other periods put together)	
		4,600 (origin of the Earth)

STRATIGRAPHICAL COLUMN
A series of Eras and Periods (and Epochs in the Cenozoic) are used to describe the age of rocks and fossils.

Turning to stone

THE PROCESS OF CHANGING from a living organism to a fossil takes place over millions of years. Fossilization is an extremely chancy process. As soon as animals and plants die, they begin to decompose, or rot. The hard parts, such as the shells, bones, and teeth of animals, or the wood of plants, last longer than soft tissue but they are often scattered by animals, wind, or flowing water. In order for something to be fossilized it must be buried quickly before it decomposes. This is most likely to be done by sediment like sand or mud washed down by water. Some fossils later dissolve; others may be changed chemically or be distorted due to high temperatures and pressures. Only a tiny fraction will survive to be found. The mussel is a good example to show how something can be fossilized.

LAND SHAPES
Over millions of years rocks are eroded and shaped, bringing ancient fossils to the surface.

2 DECAYING MUSSEL
When the mussel dies, the two chalky shells open out into a "butterfly" position. The soft parts of the mussel enclosed by the shells soon begin to rot or are eaten by scavenging animals.

Living mussel

Byssal threads

1 LIVING MUSSEL
Mussels live attached to rocks and other hard surfaces in the sea by byssal threads. The soft parts are enclosed by two chalky shells. Each individual may spend its entire life in one place, and dense masses form mussel beds. If a mussel becomes detached it may die, especially if it is swept into a different environment.

FROM PRESERVATION TO DISCOVERY

These four drawings show how animals can be preserved and their remains discovered millions of years later. It is a very slow process and the climate and shape of the land will probably change as much as the animal and plant life.

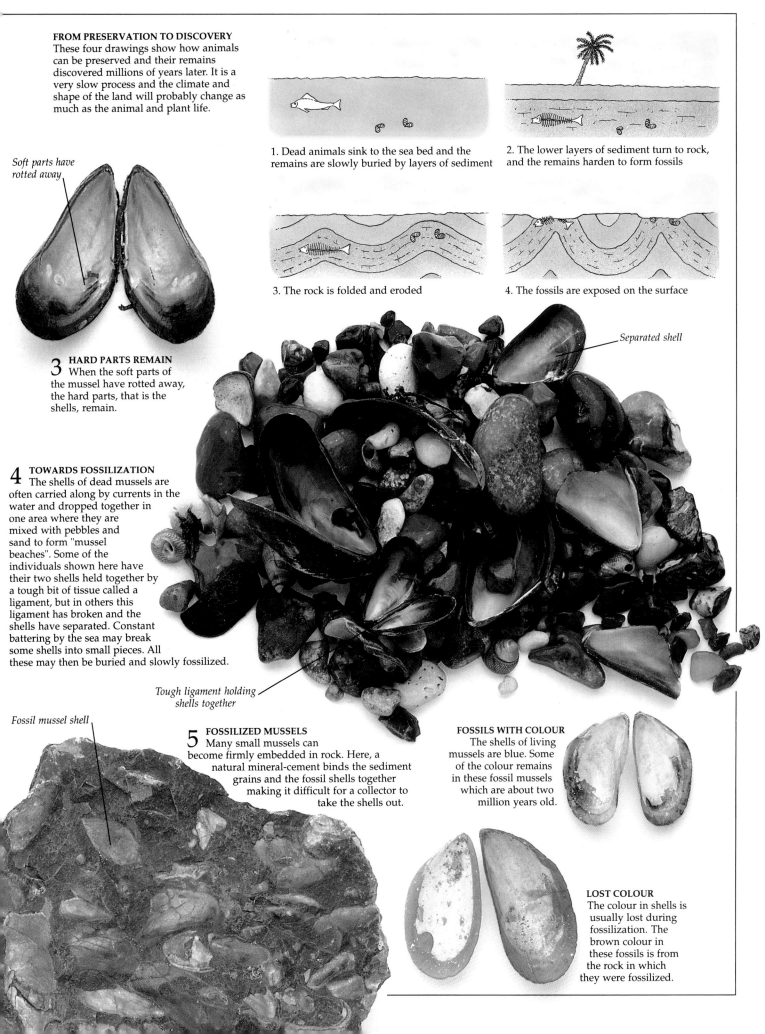

1. Dead animals sink to the sea bed and the remains are slowly buried by layers of sediment

2. The lower layers of sediment turn to rock, and the remains harden to form fossils

3. The rock is folded and eroded

4. The fossils are exposed on the surface

Soft parts have rotted away

Separated shell

3 HARD PARTS REMAIN
When the soft parts of the mussel have rotted away, the hard parts, that is the shells, remain.

4 TOWARDS FOSSILIZATION
The shells of dead mussels are often carried along by currents in the water and dropped together in one area where they are mixed with pebbles and sand to form "mussel beaches". Some of the individuals shown here have their two shells held together by a tough bit of tissue called a ligament, but in others this ligament has broken and the shells have separated. Constant battering by the sea may break some shells into small pieces. All these may then be buried and slowly fossilized.

Tough ligament holding shells together

Fossil mussel shell

5 FOSSILIZED MUSSELS
Many small mussels can become firmly embedded in rock. Here, a natural mineral-cement binds the sediment grains and the fossil shells together making it difficult for a collector to take the shells out.

FOSSILS WITH COLOUR
The shells of living mussels are blue. Some of the colour remains in these fossil mussels which are about two million years old.

LOST COLOUR
The colour in shells is usually lost during fossilization. The brown colour in these fossils is from the rock in which they were fossilized.

The changing world

THE HISTORY OF LIFE has been played out on a world which has been changing since it was formed about 4,600 million years ago (mya). The Earth's crust is divided into several plates which move relative to one another. Most earthquakes and volcanoes occur along boundaries between these plates. The combined effects of many small plate movements have caused continents to drift across the Earth, to collide and form mountains, or to break into pieces. Continents are still moving today. North America is separating from Europe at a rate of about 2 cm (0.8 in) per year. Sea levels and climates have changed many times. This is why fossils of sea-creatures can be found inland, and why fossils of tropical plants can be found where the climate is cold. The maps on these pages show the shape of the land at four stages in geological history. The fossils show a selection of the life that existed during each different time span, and many are featured later in this book.

CONTINUOUS CHANGE
The earthquakes and volcanoes of recent times, such as the great earthquake of Lisbon, Portugal, in 1755, are dramatic evidence that changes are still taking place on Earth.

THE OLDEST FOSSILS
The world's oldest fossils are minute bacteria-like cells 3,500 million years old. Complex animals made of many cells, like this *Tribrachidium* from Australia, appeared at the end of the Precambrian.

Silurian trilobites

Silurian graptolites

Silurian gastropod

Silurian brachiopods

Carboniferous mollusc (bellerophontid)

Carboniferous coral

Devonian fish

Carboniferous seed fern

Carboniferous crinoid

Gondwana

Pangaea

EARLY PALAEOZOIC WORLD (545–418 MYA)
Palaeozoic means "ancient life". During the early Palaeozoic Era (Cambrian, Ordovician, and Silurian Periods, p. 9), a large continent, known as Gondwana, was situated over the southern polar region. Most early Palaeozoic life was in the sea. Invertebrates (animals without backbones) were especially numerous, but primitive fishes were also present. Plants began to live on land towards the end of this time.

LATE PALAEOZOIC WORLD (417–249 MYA)
Life diversified greatly during the late Palaeozoic Era (Devonian, Carboniferous, and Permian Periods), at the end of which most of the land was joined in one supercontinent known as Pangaea. Amphibians, reptiles, insects, and other animals colonized the land where they could feed on the vegetation which had evolved. A mass extinction of much of the life occurred at the very end of the Palaeozoic.

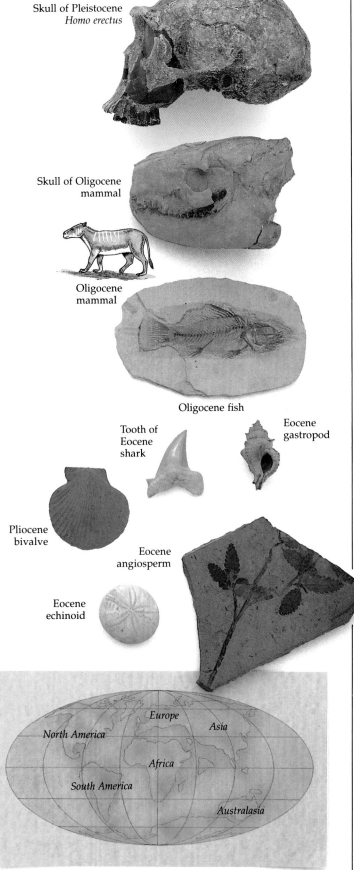

Toe bone of Cretaceous dinosaur

Cretaceous dinosaur

Skull of Pleistocene *Homo erectus*

Skull of Oligocene mammal

Oligocene mammal

Skull of Jurassic ichthyosaur

Jurassic ichthyosaur

Head of Triassic amphibian

Oligocene fish

Claw of Cretaceous dinosaur

Tooth of Eocene shark

Eocene gastropod

Twig of Jurassic conifer

Pliocene bivalve

Eocene angiosperm

Jurassic ammonite

Eocene echinoid

Cretaceous belemnite

Jurassic bivalve

MESOZOIC WORLD (248–66 MYA)

Mesozoic means "middle life". The Mesozoic Era (Cretaceous, Jurassic and Triassic Periods) is known as the Age of Reptiles. Dinosaurs stalked the land, pterosaurs swooped through the sky, and ichthyosaurs swam in the sea, with belemnites and ammonites. Flowering plants and small mammals appeared, Pangaea began to break up, and many species were wiped out in another mass extinction at the end of the Mesozoic.

CENOZOIC WORLD (65 MYA–PRESENT DAY)

The world as we know it gradually took shape during the Cenozoic Era (Palaeocene to Holocene Epochs). Cenozoic means "recent life". India moved northwards and collided with Asia, forming the Himalayas. Mammals and flowering plants became more varied and dominant on land, while teleosts (a group of bony fishes) and sea-urchins, were among groups abundant in the sea. Our own genus, *Homo,* appeared in the Pleistocene.

Early palaeontology

THE SERIOUS SCIENTIFIC STUDY OF FOSSILS began only about 300 years ago, although early Greek philosophers such as Pythagoras are reported to have realized the true nature of fossils as long ago as the 5th century B.C. During the Middle Ages in Europe, many naturalists thought fossils were the products of a mysterious "plastic force" ("*vis plastica*") which formed the fossils within the Earth. Their true origin as the buried remains of ancient animals and plants was established beyond reasonable doubt by Steno (see below) and other naturalists of the 17th century. Fossils were subsequently used to solve geological problems such as the relative ages of different rocks, and also biological problems concerning the evolution and the origin and extinction of various forms of life on Earth. Today, scientists throughout the world are still studying fossils, and our understanding of them is increasing all the time.

The frontispiece to the museum catalogue of the naturalist Johann Scheuchzer (1672–1733)

TONGUE STONES
Fossil shark teeth from Cenozoic rocks around the Mediterranean were known to naturalists as tongue stones. Some naturalists believed that they grew naturally within the rocks, but Steno and others realized their correct origins.

STENO
Niels Stensen (1638-1686), better known as Steno, was a Dane who worked as the court physician at Florence in Italy. He was one of the first people to realize the true nature of fossils, when in 1667, he noticed that the teeth of a stranded shark were very similar to tongue stones.

NOAH'S ARK
The Bible story of Noah tells how he took animals on to his ark to escape the great flood. Many naturalists, including Steno, believed that the Biblical Flood had transported and buried fossils. This explained why fossil sea-shells occurred on mountain tops. (Scheuchzer once identified the fossil of a salamander as the skeleton of a human drowned in the Flood!)

RESTORATION OF PALAEOTHERIUM
Cuvier studied *Palaeotherium* bones from the Eocene rocks of Montmartre in Paris. The animal from which they came was restored as this tapir-like mammal.

Grinding teeth of a herbivore

Fossil jaw of *Palaeotherium*

GEORGES CUVIER
The French naturalist Georges Cuvier (1769–1832) made many important contributions to natural history. Early in his scientific career he realized that the different parts of an animal's body were closely interrelated; for example, mammals with horns and hoofs were all herbivores and would have had the teeth of herbivores. The significance of this observation was that entire animals could now be restored, shown as they would have looked when alive, from the evidence of isolated bones. Cuvier also recognized that many fossils belonged to extinct species and he devised a view of Earth history in which a succession of catastrophes exterminated earlier forms of life. According to Cuvier, the last of these catastrophes was the Biblical Flood.

An 18th-century engraving of
Harvard University

Upper
Carboniferous

Lower
Carboniferous

Triassic

Lower
Jurassic

Middle
Jurassic

LOUIS AGASSIZ

Louis Agassiz (1807–1873) was a Swiss-born naturalist who emigrated to
the U.S.A. where he taught natural history at Harvard University and was
one of the first people to encourage an interest in palaeontology there. He
is especially famous for his detailed studies of fossil fishes. Agassiz was
greatly influenced by Cuvier and his catastrophe theories. He re-
interpreted some of the youngest rocks, widely believed to be deposits
formed by the Biblical Flood, and showed them to have been deposited by
glaciers during the Pleistocene Ice Age.

FIRST USEFUL MAP
William Smith, often regarded as the
father of English geology, produced the
first useful geological maps.

Gastropod

Bivalve
hinge

Gastropod

Gastropod

Bivalve

1. *Inoceramus Cuvieri. Thoms Annals V. 4 p. 448.*   4. *Ammonites.*   7. *Terebratula.*

2. *Inoceramus.*   5. *Cirrus depressus. Sowerly. M.B.*   8. *Terebratula subundata. M.C.t.15.f.7.*

3. *Cast of the inside of a Trochus.*   6. *Terebratula.*   9. *Sharks teeth.*

WILLIAM SMITH
The engineer and surveyor,
William Smith (1769–1839),
collected fossils from
different rock formations
across England. Some of
the very fossils he
collected can be seen
here, along with plates
from the books in
which he illustrated
his finds. Smith saw
that different layers of
rock were characterized
by particular species of
fossils and realized that
rocks containing the same
fossil species must
be of the same
age. Fossils are
still used today
by geologists
to work out the
relative ages of
rocks, helping
them to find
oil and other
valuable
resources.

Gastropod

Ammonite

Fig. 1 Melania Heddingtonensis Min. Con. t. 39.

2 Turbo ?

3 Trochus

Fig. 5 Chama

6 Ostrea delta Min. Con. t. 148.

7 Ammonites

Fossil folklore

FOSSILS ARE RICH IN FOLKLORE. For at least 10,000 years, fossils have figured in the beliefs, legends, and customs of ordinary people throughout the world. Even today, many people believe that particular types of fossils have supernatural or medicinal powers. Early people apparently valued particular fossils because of their rarity or natural beauty. The origin of fossils was mysterious to people for a long time and led to some peculiar ideas about them. These ideas became part of folklore, although they have surely been changed and adapted as they were passed down from generation to generation. We now know what the real origin of fossils is, but it is fascinating to see how our ancestors managed to find an explanation for them.

An artist's idea of the Devil

DEVIL'S TOENAIL
The Jurassic oyster *Gryphaea* had a thick curved shell which is still popularly known as a Devil's toenail. This explanation was given to it in spite of the fact that the Devil has usually been described as having hoofs rather than toes!

Carved snake's head

Snakestone (ammonite)

Whitby coat of arms

Ancient Whitby coin

SNAKESTONES
Ammonites (pp. 28–29) from Whitby in England were believed to be the remains of coiled snakes turned to stone by the 7th-century abbess, St Hilda. Craftsmen carved heads on to some ammonites to help with this belief. Three snakestones are included in the Whitby coat of arms, seen on this ancient coin.

Thunderstones (fossil sea-urchins)

MAGIC STONES
There are many legends about fossil sea-urchins (pp. 32–33). Some people thought they were thunderstones, fallen from the sky during a thunderstorm. They were believed to prevent milk turning sour. One type was thought to be hardened balls of froth made by entwined snakes at midsummer. The snakes tossed them in the air and if one could be caught in a cloth it had great magical powers (right).

Woodcut of 1497

TOADSTONES
The shiny, button-shaped fossil teeth of the Mesozoic fish, *Lepidotes*, (p. 35) were believed to come from within the heads of toads. This woodcut illustration from 1497 shows the supposed removal of one.

TOADSTONE MEDICINE
In Europe, during the Middle Ages, toadstones were thought to cure epilepsy and counter poison.

OLD TOAD'S TALE
To be used as medicine, toadstones had to be removed from the head of an old toad while it was alive. Old toads were supposed to eject their stones if they were placed on a red cloth. In reality, toadstones have no connection whatever with toads but the popular name is still used today for the fossil teeth of the extinct fish, *Lepidotes*.

Toadstones (fossil fish teeth)

FAMOUS MYTH
This illustration showing the mythical unicorn is a detail from a French tapestry called *The Lady and the Unicorn*, dating from about 1500.

*Unicornum verum
(fossil mammoth tusk)*

REAL UNICORN
The tusk of a small whale called the narwhal was for many years identified as the horn of the unicorn. However, the discovery in about 1600 of some fossil mammoth tusks led to these being proclaimed as the true horns of unicorns, or *unicornum verum*!

LUCKY SPINES
These are the club-shaped spines of the sea-urchin *Balanocidaris*. They can be found in Cretaceous rocks of an area in the Middle East which used to be called Judea, hence their name of Jewstones. They were used as good luck charms as long ago as B.C. 650.

*Natural hole
through sponge*

Porosphaera

SPONGE BEADS
Bronze-Age people in Britain made necklaces by stringing together certain fossil sponges. Specimens of the Cretaceous sponge *Porosphaera* can be remarkably like beads. Many even have a natural hole through the middle probably caused by the sponge having grown around part of another creature or plant.

BRONZE-AGE BURIAL
The skeletons of this woman clasping a child were found buried on Dunstable Down, England. Around the grave were three rows of fossil sea-urchins, buried with the woman and child about three thousand years ago, maybe to ward off evil spirits.

*Thunderbolts
(belemnites)*

*Stone swallow
(fossil brachiopod)*

TAKE ONE SHELL
In China the fossil shells of certain brachiopods (p. 25) are called Shiy-yen (stone swallows) and are still used as medicine. According to the prescription supplied with these Devonian brachiopods, they should be ground up, baked in a clay pot and taken as a cure for many illnesses including rheumatism, cataracts, anaemia, and digestive problems. The medicine is described as sweet and cooling.

THUNDERBOLTS
These are the internal shells of extinct squid-like animals called belemnites (p. 29). In folklore they were thought to have been flung down as darts from the heavens during thunderstorms and supposed to have medicinal powers. Belemnites have also been found with human skeletons in ancient burial mounds.

Fossils of the future

THE FOSSIL RECORD is a highly selective sample of ancient life. Many creatures did not have resistant hard parts and rotted away entirely. Some lived in environments where burial and fossilization were unlikely to occur; for example, in tree tops. Others lived in the sea, lakes, and rivers where fossilization was more likely. Yet, even in these environments, only a small proportion of life would have been fossilized. This selectivity is well illustrated by looking at a modern community to see which animals and plants might become fossils of the future.

Mackerel skeletons

TEMPORARY TENANT

A good example of a creature that is unlikely to leave direct evidence of its existence is the hermit crab. Hermit crabs are unusual in having no shell of their own. They use old snail shells as homes. In some habitats every available snail shell contains a hermit crab. Much of a hermit crab's body is soft and it twists in the spiral of the snail shell. The claws are hard but are rarely fossilized and are almost never found within the shell occupied by the crab. This is probably because decay of the organic material in the claws causes them to disintegrate before fossilization. However, when looking at fossil snail shells, it is worth bearing in mind that they may have had two tenants – a snail and a hermit crab.

Dogfish teeth   Crab shell

Scallop shells

Snail shell

Edible sea-urchin skeleton

Green sea-urchin skeleton

Common starfish skeleton   Cushion-star skeleton   Spiny starfish skeleton

Brittlestar skeleton

Bryozoan skeletons

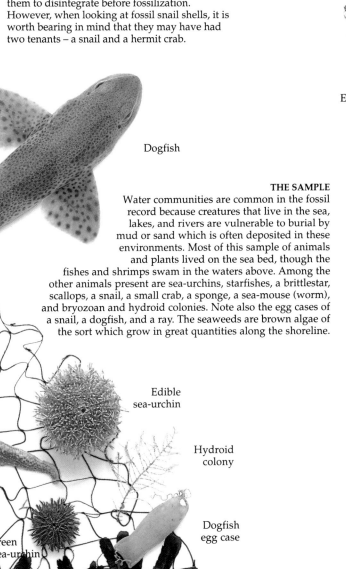

Dogfish

THE SAMPLE

Water communities are common in the fossil record because creatures that live in the sea, lakes, and rivers are vulnerable to burial by mud or sand which is often deposited in these environments. Most of this sample of animals and plants lived on the sea bed, though the fishes and shrimps swam in the waters above. Among the other animals present are sea-urchins, starfishes, a brittlestar, scallops, a snail, a small crab, a sponge, a sea-mouse (worm), and bryozoan and hydroid colonies. Note also the egg cases of a snail, a dogfish, and a ray. The seaweeds are brown algae of the sort which grow in great quantities along the shoreline.

THE REMAINS

The parts of animals that are most likely to be fossilized are the hard parts such as teeth, bones, and shells. The hard parts of the sample of animals and plants are shown together here. The seaweeds and many of the animals have disappeared entirely. Others have left very little trace. All that remains of the dogfish, for example, are its teeth. A dogfish has a skeleton of non-resistant cartilage, not bone. The sea-urchins, starfishes, brittlestar, crab, and bryozoans had resistant skeletons. However, these consisted of many separate pieces which have now mostly fallen apart as the soft tissues connecting them decayed. Only the snail and scallop shells have survived with little obvious change. The mackerel bones and crab shell would probably decay before fossilization unless buried very rapidly because they contain a lot of organic material. This illustrates dramatically how little of a modern community would usually survive to be fossilized. The same was true for communities of the geological past.

Edible sea-urchin

Hydroid colony

Dogfish egg case

Green sea-urchin

Crab

LEAVING NO TRACE

Animals and plants living and dying on land often decay completely before they can be buried and fossilized. The fur and flesh of this reindeer carcass, photographed in the Arctic, are beginning to rot away from the bones. These too will disintegrate unless by chance they are buried.

Remarkable remains

Skin traces

V ERY OCCASIONALLY, fossils of soft tissues, which usually decay during fossilization, are found. These include entirely soft-bodied animals which are otherwise unrepresented in the fossil record. Fossilization of soft parts is of great importance because it supplies much more information about the living animals than do bones, teeth, or shells. Discoveries of preserved humans are always exciting and include those at Pompeii in Italy and Grauballe in Denmark.

Part   Counterpart

IN TWO PARTS
The outline of the body is clearly shown in this fossilized frog. Even traces of the skin and other fleshy tissues have been preserved. The rock has split straight through the preserved animal, leaving the fossil in two pieces known as the part and counterpart.

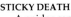

STICKY DEATH
A spider can clearly be seen in this piece of amber, the fossilized resin of an ancient plant. Amber often contains animals that were trapped in the sticky resin as it dripped down trunks and stems. Insects, spiders, and even small lizards and frogs have been preserved for millions of years in this way.

UNIQUE INFORMATION
This unusual worm is from a deposit known as the Burgess Shale in British Columbia, Canada, famous for its soft-bodied fossils. Other animals discovered in the Burgess Shale include trilobites (p. 30) with their limbs intact, primitive crustaceans and several bizarre creatures which do not fit within any groups living today. These animals were buried in mudflows on the Cambrian sea bed over 500 million years ago, and their fossils provide us with a unique glimpse of a very varied early community.

EXCEPTIONAL INSECT
This delicate dragonfly was buried in mud which formed the Solnhofen Limestone of Bavaria, West Germany, a deposit renowned for its exceptional fossils.

DEEP FROZEN MAMMOTH
Mammoths have occasionally been recovered from the permafrost (permanently frozen ground) of Siberia. They were probably trapped and frozen when they fell into crevasses in glaciers. Mammoths lived during the Ice Ages of the last two million years, becoming extinct about 12,000 years ago. The largest species grew to over 4 m (13 ft) at the shoulder.

ACTIVE VOLCANO
The famous volcano Vesuvius in Italy, has erupted frequently. It has been quiet since 1944 but is not thought to be extinct.

Cast of body from Pompeii

BURIED IN ASH
During the violent eruption of Mount Vesuvius in A.D. 79, inhabitants of the nearby towns of Pompeii and Herculaneum were buried beneath avalanches of volcanic ash and debris before they could escape. The bodies lasted long enough for the ash to harden around them and when they decayed they left cavities. The gruesome shapes of victims' bodies have been revealed by filling excavated cavities with plaster to give casts. Some skeletons of pets have also been found.

SOFT PRESERVATION *left*

Belemnoteuthis from the Jurassic is related to squid, cuttlefish, and the extinct belemnites (p. 29). The internal skeleton of this specimen is hidden beneath the soft body which has been preserved because of replacement by the mineral apatite soon after death and burial. Even the hooked tentacles around the head can be seen. Ink was released from a sac as a defensive screen, an ability its relatives possess today.

Hooked tentacles

Preserved soft body hides the internal skeleton

The cast of the body shows exactly how this person was lying when buried by ash over 1,900 years ago

Bone

Skin

Fossil moa foot

SKINNY CLAW

The moas of New Zealand were large flightless birds related to the kiwi, emu, and ostrich. The biggest was 3.5 m (11 ft) tall. Although now extinct, moas were alive when Maoris first lived in New Zealand 700 years ago. Fossils of many different species of moa have been found, some over two million years old. This fossilized foot still has skin attached. The impact these once dominant birds had on New Zealand's native vegetation is still evident today in plants that have evolved a resistance to being eaten by moas!

Claw

A moa among kiwis

Reconstruction of a mammoth stuck in the tar at La Brea

STUCK FAST

Tar oozing naturally to the surface at La Brea in Los Angeles, U.S.A., has entombed many animals accidentally caught in the sticky substance over the past 10,000 to 20,000 years. Excavations in the older solidified layers of tar have unearthed the bones of extinct mammals such as mammoths and sabretooth cats (p. 55).

GRAUBALLE MAN

Human bodies in remarkable states of preservation have been excavated from several peat bogs in northern Europe. The acid material of the bogs prevented the total decay of soft parts. Many bodies are over 2,000 years old and some show signs of a ritual killing. This man was found in 1952 near the village of Grauballe in Denmark. He died in about the 4th century. Even skin and internal organs, including remains of his last meal, have been preserved.

Corals

Corals are some of the most beautiful animals in the sea. The colourful massed tentacles of coral individuals, or polyps, resemble flowers in an undersea garden. Most corals live in warm, shallow, tropical waters and feed on plankton but also obtain nutrition from algae which may live within their bodies. Corals may be solitary (living by themselves) or colonial (many polyps joined together). Fossil corals are common because beneath the soft-bodied polyps are hard chalky skeletons. The oldest are from the Ordovician. Related sea-anemones and jellyfish lack hard skeletons and are seldom fossilized.

CORAL FISHING
Coral has long been collected for its beauty and is used in jewellery.

Separate corallite

A ring-shaped coral reef is called an atoll

Individual coral skeleton

Red limestone

PIPE CORAL
The pipe-shaped corallites (skeletons formed by individual polyps) of this Carboniferous coral colony, *Lithostrotion*, grew separately. The spaces between them are now filled with red limestone.

HORN CORAL
Aulophyllum, shown here in two pieces, is a typical solitary coral. The coral lived on the sea bed growing in this characteristic horn shape. The pointed end was buried in sediment on the sea bed and the soft polyp sat on top of the other end.

PACKED COLONY
This colonial coral, *Lonsdaleia*, belongs to a group called the Rugosa. Rugose corals became extinct in the Permian. The individual corallites which make up the colony are many-sided, usually hexagonal (six-sided), because they are so tightly packed together.

MODERN CORALS
Most modern corals belong to a group called the scleractinians which first appeared in the Triassic. Coral reefs are inhabited by countless animals and are the most diverse marine environments.

Pale sediment filling areas once occupied by soft tissues

Branch of corallites

CHAIN CORAL
This Silurian coral, *Halysites*, has corallites arranged in long branching ribbons. On the surface, it looks like a collection of chains.

Winding valley of coral

BRAIN CORAL
Together, the individuals of brain corals form winding valleys and the colonies resemble human brains. Polyps may share a common mouth with others in the same valley. This Miocene example has been cut horizontally and polished to show the inside.

CORAL BUSH
Colonies of this coral, *Thamnopora*, are bush-shaped with corallites opening all over the surfaces of the branches. This example, in a piece of limestone, has been cut across horizontally and polished to show the shape of the colony.

RECORD-BREAKING CORAL
This fossilized fragment of coral is the reef-building coral *Galaxea*. The structure of the individual skeletons can easily be seen. The world's largest known living coral is a *Galaxea* colony from Okinawa in Japan. It has a circumference of 16 m (52 ft).

Individual coral skeleton

Fossil Fungia

SOLITARY CORALS
These unusual-looking fossils are the delicate skeletons of the solitary corals *Stephanophyllia* and *Fungia*, which lived on the sea bed in the Pliocene and Pleistocene respectively. As their name suggests, the skeletons of *Fungia* look like the undersides of mushrooms.

Fossil Stephanophyllia

Skeleton replaced by silica

REPLACED CORAL
Some fossil corals have skeletons made of the mineral aragonite. This dissolves easily, so the skeletons often disappear during fossilization. In this fossil colony of *Thecosmilia* the skeletons have been replaced by silica.

Sea bed dwellers

AMONG THE COMMONEST FOSSILS to be found are the remains of animals and plants which lived on the sea bed. They lived where sand and mud was regularly deposited and most of the animals had hard parts which could survive decay and be fossilized. The plants and many of the animals could not escape burial, even when they were alive, because they lacked the ability to move. Bryozoans and brachiopods are living examples of this type of animal but because they live in the sea, not many people are aware of their existence. Today, there are only 250 known species of brachiopods. This contrasts with the huge numbers – about 30,000 – of known fossil species.

CLOSE NEIGHBOURS
Bryozoan colonies can be compared to blocks of flats and other buildings containing several similar homes.

Holes in the colony through which water and food particles are pumped

ARCHIMEDES SCREW
This distinctive Carboniferous bryozoan is named after a spiral water pump invented by the Greek philosopher Archimedes. The screw-shaped skeleton once supported a twisted net of individuals similar to *Hornera* (centre left).

Archimedes' water pump

Each piece is a colony containing at least 200 individuals

COMMUNITY HOMES *above*
Because of their branching shape, this type of modern bryozoan, *Hornera*, often provides a home for worms, small fishes, and many other animals in the sea.

One individual skeleton

LARGER THAN LIFE
The calcite skeletons of individuals in a bryozoan colony are magnified here many times.

Calcite colonies

Bryozoans are tiny animals which live in colonies where each individual is attached to its neighbour. A colony may contain tens, hundreds or even thousands of individuals, each one less than 1 mm (0.04 in) long. They have tentacles which they use to feed on tiny particles of food. Most have calcite skeletons. Colonies grow by budding new individuals and vary in shape. Some are flat sheets; others grow upright and can look like nets or bushes.

Light and dark growth bands

Free-living colonies of Cretaceous bryozoans

OLD LACE
The fragments of lace bryozoan (*Chasmatopora*) in this Ordovician shale are among the oldest known bryozoans.

BEETROOT STONE
The red colour of this Jurassic alga, *Solenopora*, is sometimes preserved and these fossils are then known as beetroot stones.

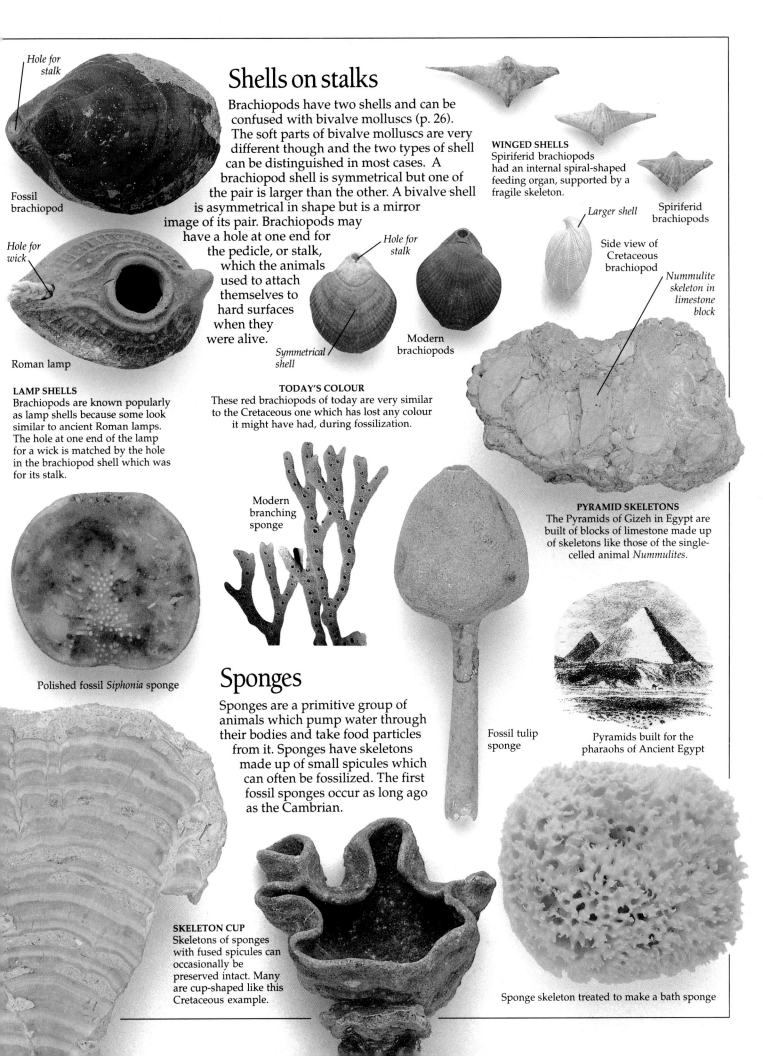

Shells on stalks

Brachiopods have two shells and can be confused with bivalve molluscs (p. 26). The soft parts of bivalve molluscs are very different though and the two types of shell can be distinguished in most cases. A brachiopod shell is symmetrical but one of the pair is larger than the other. A bivalve shell is asymmetrical in shape but is a mirror image of its pair. Brachiopods may have a hole at one end for the pedicle, or stalk, which the animals used to attach themselves to hard surfaces when they were alive.

Hole for stalk

Fossil brachiopod

Hole for wick

Roman lamp

Hole for stalk

Symmetrical shell

Modern brachiopods

WINGED SHELLS
Spiriferid brachiopods had an internal spiral-shaped feeding organ, supported by a fragile skeleton.

Larger shell

Spiriferid brachiopods

Side view of Cretaceous brachiopod

Nummulite skeleton in limestone block

LAMP SHELLS
Brachiopods are known popularly as lamp shells because some look similar to ancient Roman lamps. The hole at one end of the lamp for a wick is matched by the hole in the brachiopod shell which was for its stalk.

TODAY'S COLOUR
These red brachiopods of today are very similar to the Cretaceous one which has lost any colour it might have had, during fossilization.

PYRAMID SKELETONS
The Pyramids of Gizeh in Egypt are built of blocks of limestone made up of skeletons like those of the single-celled animal *Nummulites*.

Modern branching sponge

Polished fossil *Siphonia* sponge

Sponges

Sponges are a primitive group of animals which pump water through their bodies and take food particles from it. Sponges have skeletons made up of small spicules which can often be fossilized. The first fossil sponges occur as long ago as the Cambrian.

Fossil tulip sponge

Pyramids built for the pharaohs of Ancient Egypt

SKELETON CUP
Skeletons of sponges with fused spicules can occasionally be preserved intact. Many are cup-shaped like this Cretaceous example.

Sponge skeleton treated to make a bath sponge

Shells of all shapes

AT THE BEGINNING of the Cambrian Period, about 545 million years ago, complex animals with hard shells and skeletons first appeared in the sea. Among these were the molluscs, a group of animals which are still abundant today. Gastropods, or snails, and bivalves such as clams, mussels, and oysters are the most familiar molluscs but other kinds include chitons and cephalopods (p. 29). Bivalves have two shells, or valves, joined together by a hinge, whereas gastropods only have one shell. The shells of molluscs are often found as fossils. Most are made of calcite, or of aragonite which dissolves more easily. Internal moulds of molluscs are often found because aragonite shells may become filled with sediment and the shells themselves dissolved.

VENUS'S SHELL
The goddess Venus depicted emerging from a scallop shell.

Pearl

ANCIENT JEWELS
This mudstone contains rare fossil pearls. From the Eocene, they are about 50 million years old.

Hinge tooth

Muscle scar

HINGED TOGETHER
Hinge teeth helped hold a bivalve's shells together when it was alive. This shell belonged to an Eocene bivalve, *Venericardia*.

Shell *Eye*

Gape

Sensory tentacles

GOOD EYESIGHT
Scallops have many eyes, each with well-developed focussing lenses. They are situated in soft tissue near the edge of the shells. Scallops can open their shells which are hinged together. To feed, they use their gills to cause a current of water, laden with food particles to pass through the gape in the shells.

SPINES FOR SPONGES
The "thorny oyster" *Spondylus* is so named because of its spiny shell, as seen in this Pliocene specimen. Spines of modern *Spondylus* help sponges and other encrusting animals to grow on their shells, so protecting the bivalve from predators.

Prominent rib

FALLING APART
These fossilized shells, one flat, the other convex (domed), belong to the scallop, *Pecten*, from the Pliocene. The prominent ribs on the two shells interlock, but, as with many bivalve fossils, the shells are usually found separated because the connecting ligament decomposes.

CARVED IN STONE
These unusual fossils have an ancient Arabic prayer carved on them. They are internal casts (p. 6) of bivalves, formed by sediment which solidified in the space between the shells.

Modern Cone
shell

Fossil Cone
shell

Modern snail shell

Fossil snail shells

DISAPPEARING COLOUR
Some living gastropods,
especially those of the tropics, are
often very brightly coloured.
Their colour is due to pigment, a
chemical substance within the
shell. Unfortunately, pigments are
usually destroyed during
fossilization.

Siphon

Foot

SOFT-HEARTED
This modern sea-
snail is just emerging
from its shell. Parts
of its soft body can
clearly be seen
(at top and
bottom right).

Modern snail

Curious coils

Gastropod shells of all ages
come in many different shapes
and sizes. They are all open at
one end with a gradually
increasing diameter and are
usually twisted into a spiral
coil. The exact shape of the
spiral varies according to the
species. It can be left-handed,
right-handed, loosely coiled
or tightly coiled, regular or
irregular. The freshwater
snail *Planorbis* has a shell
where the coiling is almost
flat. *Turritella* has a shell
which is drawn out into a
high spire.

Spiral coil

Fossil
Turritella

"WORM SHELLS"
Vermetids are unusual
gastropods as they attach
themselves permanently to a hard surface,
often in clusters like these fossil examples.
Their shells are irregularly coiled and look
more like worms.

Fossil chiton

Modern
chiton

NO CONNECTION
Chitons are a small group of marine
molluscs with shells made up of
eight individual plates. Fossil
chitons are rare and their plates are
disconnected. Today, chitons can be
found in rock pools sticking to the
sides of the rocks from which they
scrape algae for food.

LOOSE COILS
Tubina is a very
unusual type of
mollusc which
belonged to a
now extinct
group called the
bellerophontids.
It has a loosely
coiled shell and
dates from the
Devonian Period.
It is uncertain whether it was a true
gastropod or not because its soft
body has not been preserved.

Left-handed coil

Right-handed coil

SPIRAL FOSSILS
Most gastropods have
shells with a right-
handed spiral coil, like
Neptunea despecta, but the
shell of *Neptunea contraria*
has a left-handed coil.

Fossil *Neptunea*
contraria

Fossil *Neptunea*
despecta

Siphonal canal

**EXTRA
LONG**
The pointed
shell of *Fusinus*
is further
lengthened by
a siphonal
canal which the
animal
used in respiration.

Top

Fossil *Planorbis*

Underneath

Intelligent molluscs

An ammonite with its shell partly replaced by iron pyrites

THE OCTOPUS, SQUID, and cuttlefish are modern representatives of a group of sea-dwelling molluscs called cephalopods which have left a rich fossil record. Cephalopods are regarded as the most highly developed molluscs. They have suckered tentacles, eyes that are remarkably similar to more advanced vertebrate animals, and the ability to learn and use their learning. They are active predators moving quickly through the water using a type of jet propulsion. Most modern cephalopods have shells completely covered by soft parts. However, like the living *Nautilus*, many fossil cephalopods, including the ammonites had external shells rather like the shells of snails but divided into chambers. Following their first appearance in the Cambrian, many different species of cephalopods came and went, making them very useful fossils for dating rocks (p. 9).

IMPORTANT EVIDENCE
As the only living Nautiloid, *Nautilus* is the closest modern relative of the ammonites, and provides us with important clues about this extinct group. *Nautilus* is a nocturnal animal, active only at night, and lives in the Pacific Ocean at depths ranging from about 5–550 m (16–1,800 ft). Its prey consists of fish and crustaceans which it eats using its hard beak.

DECORATIVE MOTIF
The beautiful shape of ammonites is often used in decoration. This is a column from a terraced house in Brighton, England. The architect's name was Amon!

Septa dividing shell into chambers

Final chamber

Complex suture line

Ammonites

VARIOUS SIZES
Some Mesozoic ammonites reached gigantic sizes. This large specimen, about 30 cm (12 in) wide, is small compared to giants which could be 2 m (6ft 6in) in diameter.

Simple suture line

Fossil nautiloids

ROOMS FOR EXPANSION
Fossil ammonites and nautiloids have coiled shells divided into a series of chambers by septa. Only the final chamber next to the opening was occupied by the animal. As it grew, the animal periodically moved forwards and formed new septa at the rear of the body chamber. Older chambers were filled with liquid and gas, the proportions of which could be changed through a canal called the siphuncle to allow the animal to move up and down in the sea. Suture lines, formed where the septa meet the shell, are simple in nautiloids but are folded into complex saddles and lobes in ammonites.

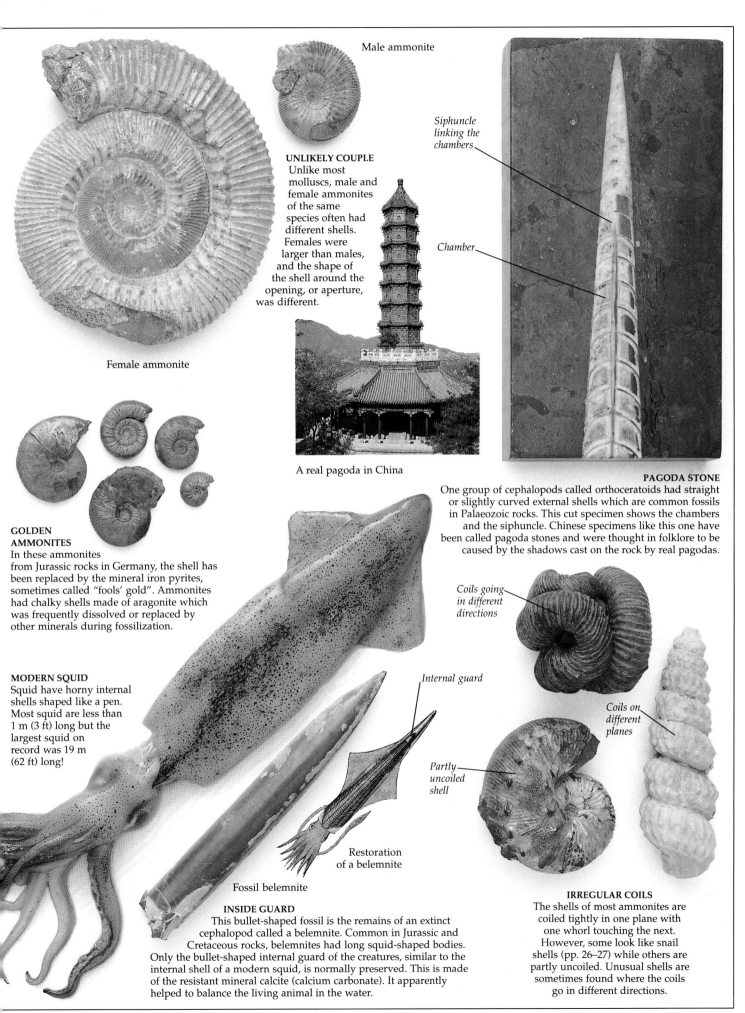

Male ammonite

Female ammonite

UNLIKELY COUPLE
Unlike most molluscs, male and female ammonites of the same species often had different shells. Females were larger than males, and the shape of the shell around the opening, or aperture, was different.

Siphuncle linking the chambers

Chamber

A real pagoda in China

PAGODA STONE
One group of cephalopods called orthoceratoids had straight or slightly curved external shells which are common fossils in Palaeozoic rocks. This cut specimen shows the chambers and the siphuncle. Chinese specimens like this one have been called pagoda stones and were thought in folklore to be caused by the shadows cast on the rock by real pagodas.

GOLDEN AMMONITES
In these ammonites from Jurassic rocks in Germany, the shell has been replaced by the mineral iron pyrites, sometimes called "fools' gold". Ammonites had chalky shells made of aragonite which was frequently dissolved or replaced by other minerals during fossilization.

MODERN SQUID
Squid have horny internal shells shaped like a pen. Most squid are less than 1 m (3 ft) long but the largest squid on record was 19 m (62 ft) long!

Internal guard

Coils going in different directions

Coils on different planes

Partly uncoiled shell

Restoration of a belemnite

Fossil belemnite

INSIDE GUARD
This bullet-shaped fossil is the remains of an extinct cephalopod called a belemnite. Common in Jurassic and Cretaceous rocks, belemnites had long squid-shaped bodies. Only the bullet-shaped internal guard of the creatures, similar to the internal shell of a modern squid, is normally preserved. This is made of the resistant mineral calcite (calcium carbonate). It apparently helped to balance the living animal in the water.

IRREGULAR COILS
The shells of most ammonites are coiled tightly in one plane with one whorl touching the next. However, some look like snail shells (pp. 26–27) while others are partly uncoiled. Unusual shells are sometimes found where the coils go in different directions.

29

Animals in armour

INSECTS, SPIDERS, CRABS, SCORPIONS, lobsters, millipedes, barnacles, and many other animals all belong to a major group of animals called the arthropods, a word which means "jointed foot". Arthropods are an extremely varied group with species adapted to living in the sea, on the land, and in the air but many are not commonly found as fossils. They all have jointed legs, a segmented body, and an exoskeleton, or outer armour. As the animal grows, it has to shed its exoskeleton every so often and grow another one. Some arthropods, for example, the extinct trilobites, have the mineral calcite in their exoskeletons, making them resistant to decay. These exoskeletons are the parts of arthropods most commonly found fossilized.

SMALL IS BEAUTIFUL
Most trilobites were 3–10 cm (1–4 in) long. These are examples of *Elrathia*.

PRIZE POSSESSION
Trilobites are prized fossils. This Silurian *Calymene* has been made into a brooch. Examples of this species were found at Dudley, England, in such great numbers that they were nicknamed Dudley bugs.

TO SEE OR NOT TO SEE?
There were more than 10,000 different species of trilobites and all of them lived in the sea. Some crawled along the sea bed, others floated or swam through the water. Most species had two eyes and could probably see very well. Lenses are sometimes preserved in fossil trilobites because they were made of the resistant mineral calcite. Some species however were eyeless. Most of these lived in the deep sea, beyond the depth to which natural light penetrates.

No eyes

Eye

Trilobite *Dalmanites*

Trilobite *Concoryphe*

Modern millipede

Fossil millipede

EARLY SETTLERS
Like all arthropods, millipedes have bodies divided into pieces or segments. Unlike the other arthropods on these pages, they live on land. Seldom found as fossils, they were one of the first animals to live on land.

Packed lenses

MULTI-VISION
Trilobite eyes are the most ancient visual systems known. They consisted of many separate lenses packed together. Each lens produced its own image.

Echinocaris, a Devonian shrimp-like arthropod

ROLL UP!
Some trilobites were able to roll up like woodlice, probably for protection against predators.

TRI-LOBED
The name trilobite was given to these creatures because their exoskeletons are divided into three distinct parts or lobes. The legs on the lower surface of the animal and the soft parts were very rarely preserved. Whole fossil trilobites are surprisingly rare but they can be found in rocks from the Cambrian to the Permian Period, about 545 to 248 million years old. They became extinct after that. This one is *Paradoxides* from the Cambrian. One of the biggest of all trilobites, it grew to 50 cm (1ft 7in) long.

Long spine

PRICKLY CUSTOMER
This Devonian trilobite, *Dicranurus*, was notable for its long spines which are superbly preserved in this specimen.

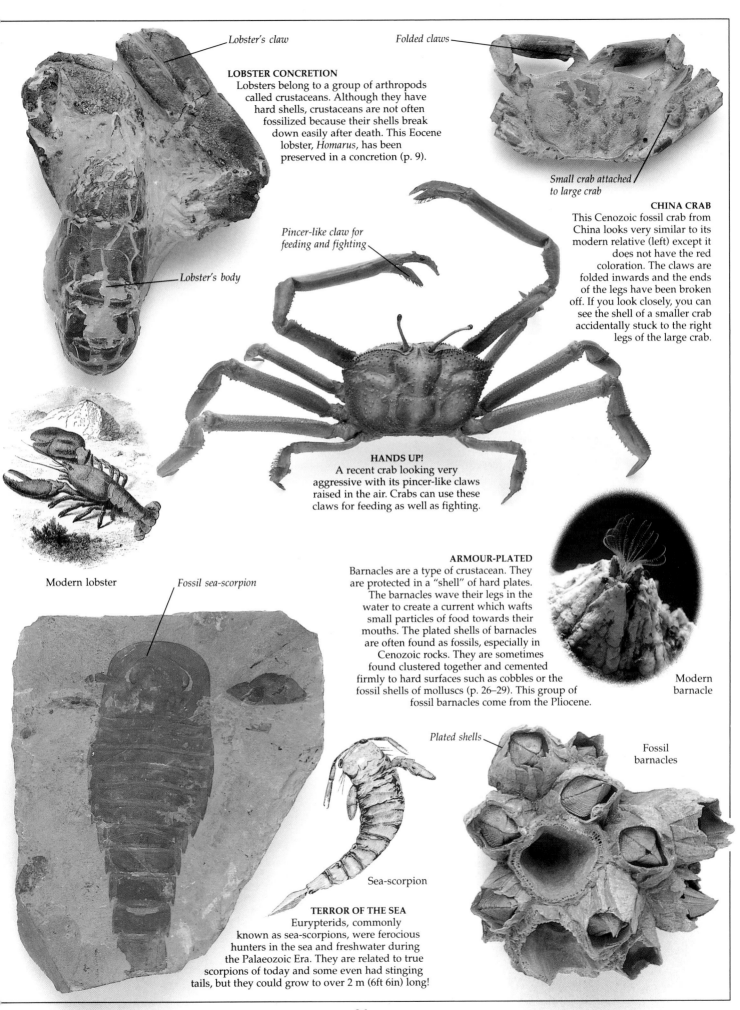

Lobster's claw

LOBSTER CONCRETION
Lobsters belong to a group of arthropods called crustaceans. Although they have hard shells, crustaceans are not often fossilized because their shells break down easily after death. This Eocene lobster, _Homarus_, has been preserved in a concretion (p. 9).

Folded claws

Small crab attached to large crab

CHINA CRAB
This Cenozoic fossil crab from China looks very similar to its modern relative (left) except it does not have the red coloration. The claws are folded inwards and the ends of the legs have been broken off. If you look closely, you can see the shell of a smaller crab accidentally stuck to the right legs of the large crab.

Pincer-like claw for feeding and fighting

Lobster's body

HANDS UP!
A recent crab looking very aggressive with its pincer-like claws raised in the air. Crabs can use these claws for feeding as well as fighting.

Modern lobster

Fossil sea-scorpion

ARMOUR-PLATED
Barnacles are a type of crustacean. They are protected in a "shell" of hard plates. The barnacles wave their legs in the water to create a current which wafts small particles of food towards their mouths. The plated shells of barnacles are often found as fossils, especially in Cenozoic rocks. They are sometimes found clustered together and cemented firmly to hard surfaces such as cobbles or the fossil shells of molluscs (p. 26–29). This group of fossil barnacles come from the Pliocene.

Modern barnacle

Plated shells

Fossil barnacles

Sea-scorpion

TERROR OF THE SEA
Eurypterids, commonly known as sea-scorpions, were ferocious hunters in the sea and freshwater during the Palaeozoic Era. They are related to true scorpions of today and some even had stinging tails, but they could grow to over 2 m (6ft 6in) long!

Arms and spines

ECHINODERMS are a very distinctive group of animals which all live in the sea. Among them are sea-urchins (echinoids), sea-lilies (crinoids), starfish (asteroids), and brittlestars (ophiuroids). The distinguishing feature of most echinoderms is their five-fold radial symmetry. That is, their bodies can be divided into five similar segments, rather like the segments of an orange. As echinoderms have skeletons made of resistant calcite they are very often found fossilized. Indeed, fossil echinoderms range back to the Cambrian. Echinoderm skeletons consist of many individual pieces or plates, each grown as a single crystal of calcite. These are often separated and scattered soon after the animal dies, so rapid burial is especially important to ensure good preservation.

Modern brittlestar

Interlinked delicate arms

BURIED ALIVE
This exceptional Jurassic specimen shows a group of five fossil brittlestars with arms interlinked. These may have been buried as they lived, as the plated skeletons are normally scattered soon after death. Brittlestars look like starfish but are more delicate and their arms break off easily - hence their name. They use their arms to move across the sea bed. Some feed on plankton but others are scavengers.

Symmetrical arm

Modern *Protoreaster*

STAR HUNTER
Many starfish are very efficient hunters, often feeding on bivalves which they open using the suckers on their arms. Others, like this Australian *Protoreaster*, extract their food from sediments such as sand.

STAR OF THE BEACH
Starfish are familiar to anyone who has explored rock pools and beaches by the sea, but they are very seldom found as fossils.

Position of missing arm

Mouth

Ammonite

Mouth

Suckers

Underside of modern starfish

ARM ROBBERY
This fossil starfish from the Jurassic, seen from underneath, is remarkably similar to some present-day species but unfortunately one of its arms is missing. Its mouth can be seen in the centre. The rock in which it is embedded contains small ammonites and many shell fragments as well.

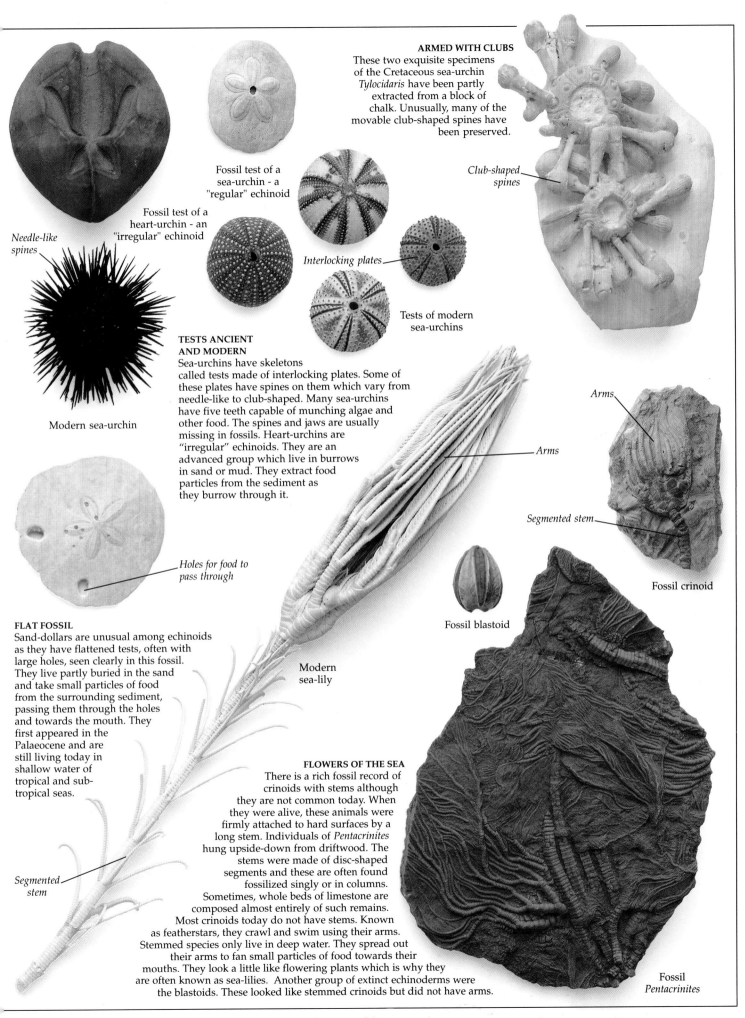

ARMED WITH CLUBS
These two exquisite specimens of the Cretaceous sea-urchin *Tylocidaris* have been partly extracted from a block of chalk. Unusually, many of the movable club-shaped spines have been preserved.

Club-shaped spines

Fossil test of a sea-urchin - a "regular" echinoid

Fossil test of a heart-urchin - an "irregular" echinoid

Needle-like spines

Interlocking plates

Tests of modern sea-urchins

Modern sea-urchin

TESTS ANCIENT AND MODERN
Sea-urchins have skeletons called tests made of interlocking plates. Some of these plates have spines on them which vary from needle-like to club-shaped. Many sea-urchins have five teeth capable of munching algae and other food. The spines and jaws are usually missing in fossils. Heart-urchins are "irregular" echinoids. They are an advanced group which live in burrows in sand or mud. They extract food particles from the sediment as they burrow through it.

Holes for food to pass through

Arms

Arms

Segmented stem

Fossil crinoid

FLAT FOSSIL
Sand-dollars are unusual among echinoids as they have flattened tests, often with large holes, seen clearly in this fossil. They live partly buried in the sand and take small particles of food from the surrounding sediment, passing them through the holes and towards the mouth. They first appeared in the Palaeocene and are still living today in shallow water of tropical and sub-tropical seas.

Modern sea-lily

Fossil blastoid

Segmented stem

FLOWERS OF THE SEA
There is a rich fossil record of crinoids with stems although they are not common today. When they were alive, these animals were firmly attached to hard surfaces by a long stem. Individuals of *Pentacrinites* hung upside-down from driftwood. The stems were made of disc-shaped segments and these are often found fossilized singly or in columns. Sometimes, whole beds of limestone are composed almost entirely of such remains. Most crinoids today do not have stems. Known as featherstars, they crawl and swim using their arms. Stemmed species only live in deep water. They spread out their arms to fan small particles of food towards their mouths. They look a little like flowering plants which is why they are often known as sea-lilies. Another group of extinct echinoderms were the blastoids. These looked like stemmed crinoids but did not have arms.

Fossil *Pentacrinites*

Fishes

FISHES are the most primitive vertebrates (animals with backbones). They are a very varied group, with about 20,000 species, which use gills to breathe and fins to swim. Some fishes live in the sea, some in freshwater, while others migrate between these environments. Fishes first appeared about 500 million years ago. Most were small, jawless, and covered with heavy armour. In the Devonian Period, often referred to as the Age of Fishes, fishes became numerous, and early representatives of the major living groups were present. Skeletons of fossil fishes can be abundant in certain areas but it is more common to find isolated teeth, especially of sharks.

Sparnodus part

FIN SPINE
Sharks and rays have skeletons made of cartilage which is softer than bone and not normally fossilized. However, they have resistant teeth and spines, and fossils of these stretch back to the Devonian. This is the spine of a Jurassic shark. It supported a large fin on the shark's back.

Dorsal fin

Impression of a modern shark

Sharp teeth

Teeth of an Eocene sand shark, *Eugomphodus*

ARMOURED FISHES
One of the first known fishes with jaws was a group of armoured fishes called placoderms. Some used their two arms to prop themselves up on the beds of rivers and freshwater lakes.

TOOTH FOR A TOOTH
Most sharks are fierce predators with a mass of sharp teeth arranged in whorls. New teeth are growing all the time to replace older teeth which drop out. The largest modern shark on record, a great white, was 9 m (29 ft 6 in) long. This is small in comparison with its extinct relative, *Carcharodon*, whose tooth (right) is 11 cm (4 in) long suggesting a body length of over 12 m (39 ft).

Tooth of Pliocene shark, *Carcharadon*

Modern ray

Ptychodus tooth

Ridges for crushing food

Ridged *Ptychodus* tooth

JAWLESS FISHES
Cephalaspids were primitive freshwater fishes. They were jawless and fed by sucking sediment from lake or river beds.

SHELL CRUSHERS
Fossil teeth like these are all that is known of a cartilaginous fish, *Ptychodus*, which was probably similar to a modern ray. It had ridged teeth, which it used to crush the shells of the molluscs on which it fed.

Well-preserved skeleton

FISH EATS FISH *right*
Fossils seldom provide direct evidence of an animal's diet. However, this remarkable Cretaceous dogfish contains the head of a teleost which it swallowed. The dogfish had very small teeth and would probably not have been able to bite the head off the body of a live fish. It seems more likely that the dogfish scavenged the head from a dead fish.

Swallowed fish head

Sparnodus counterpart

TWO PARTS
This slab of Eocene limestone has split through a fine fossil specimen of *Sparnodus*. The two bits are called the part (left) and the counterpart (above). Bones of the skeleton, including the fins, are preserved in remarkable detail. *Sparnodus* belongs to a group of bony fishes still living today known as porgies or sea-breams.

Thick scales covering the body

THICK-SCALED FISH
Lepidotes was a Mesozoic bony fish. It was common all over the world and some examples grew to a length of almost 2 m (6 ft 6 in). The body was covered by thick scales, and the button-shaped teeth, called toadstones in folklore (p. 16), were probably used to crush mollusc shells.

Sharp predator's teeth

EAR STONES
Otoliths are balance organs from the ears of fishes. They are made of chalky material and form unusual fossils. These examples are from Eocene fishes.

Modern African lungfish

Thick scales

TEETH FOR HUNTING
Related to the modern bow-fin, *Caturus* is from the Jurassic. By the look of its sharp teeth it was a predator.

Armoured head

Remains of concretion

BONY FISHES
About 200 million years ago, this primitive teleost, a type of bony fish, lived in the seas. It had small teeth which suggest that it fed on minute plankton, possibly living in shoals like the modern herring. Teleosts first appeared in the Triassic, and today they are the most common fishes. They include carp, salmon, cod, mackerel, plaice, and many others.

EXPOSED WITH ACID
Unlike modern lungfishes, which live in freshwater, the Devonian lungfish, *Chirodipterus*, lived in shallow seas. It had thick bony scales and an armoured head. This specimen from Australia was preserved in a hard chalky concretion (p. 9) and has been exposed by treatment in acid which dissolved the concretion but not the fish within.

Plants-the pioneers

THE INVASION OF THE LAND BY PLANTS about 440 million years ago was a key event in the history of life. It paved the way for colonization by animals and was the starting point for the development of the variety of plants we see today. Plants growing on the land had to be strong enough to support themselves against gravity, resistant to drying, and be able to transport water, gathered by the roots, up to the higher portions of the plant where energy-producing photosynthesis occurred. These adaptations were first seen among the primitive land plants such as clubmosses, horsetails, and ferns of the late Palaeozoic. Examples from all of these groups are living today, though often in greatly reduced numbers. The flowering plants which dominate modern floras did not appear until the Cretaceous.

JET JEWELLERY
Jet is a special kind of fossil wood which is dense enough to be carved and polished for jewellery. The formation of jet probably occurred when wood from monkey puzzle trees (opposite) was washed into the sea by rivers.

Impression in sandstone of the bark of *Lepidodendron*

JOHANN SCHEUCHZER
The Swiss naturalist and physician Johann Scheuchzer (1672–1733) studied fossil plants and fishes from the Miocene rocks at Oeningen in Switzerland.

Diamond-shaped leaf-scars

Lepidodendron

Cross-section of the fossil cone *Lepidostrobus*

Fossil *Baragwanathia*

Carboniferous clubmoss *Archaeosigillaria*

Clubmosses

Clubmosses, which belong to a group of plants called lycopods, reproduce by spores held in cones. Lycopods were common during the Palaeozoic, and *Baragwanathia* from the Devonian of Australia is probably the oldest known example. Some modern clubmosses have creeping stems but the Palaeozoic lycopods grew as trees. *Lepidodendron* reached 40 m (130 ft) tall. The fossil bark of *Lepidodendron* has a diamond pattern on it made by scars left when the leaves fell off. The fossil cones of *Lepidodendron* have been named *Lepidostrobus*.

Modern clubmoss *Lycopodium*

Archaeopteris, an extinct tree which reproduced by spores and grew up to 30 m (98 ft) tall

Towards the seeds

The oldest ferns are of Devonian age. Whereas clubmosses declined after the Palaeozoic, ferns did not. They are common fossils in Mesozoic rocks and about 10,000 species are alive today. They have spore cases on the underside of their leaves. Tree ferns such as *Psaronius* grew alongside clubmoss trees in the Coal Measure swamps. Most modern tree ferns are not closely related to these Palaeozoic forms but belong to two families which appeared in the Jurassic. The leaves of the now-extinct seed ferns often resemble true fern leaves but they were, in fact, relatives of more advanced, seed-bearing plants (pp. 38–39).

Modern fern

COMPRESSED FERN
Carbonized (turned to coal) leaves of the Jurassic fern *Coniopteris* are here preserved as compressions.

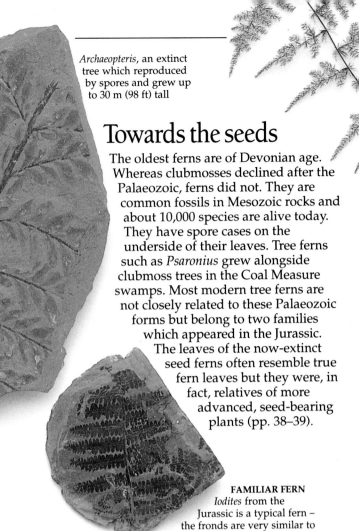

FAMILIAR FERN
Iodites from the Jurassic is a typical fern – the fronds are very similar to many modern species.

Plants in a typical Palaeozoic scene

POLISHED FERN
This sectioned and polished piece of fossil wood is from the tree fern *Psaronius*, which grew to a height of 8 m (26 ft).

FOSSIL MONKEY PUZZLE CONES
One cone has been sectioned to show the internal structure.

WIDESPREAD SEED FERN
The presence of fossils of this seed fern, *Glossopteris*, in India, Africa, South America, Australia, and Antarctica, provides evidence that these areas were once linked together as Gondwana (pp. 12–13).

The only modern horsetail genus, *Equisetum*, which grows to about 1.5 m (5 ft) tall

Leathery leaf

Modern monkey puzzle branch

MONKEY PUZZLE
The monkey puzzle is a primitive type of conifer (pp. 38–39) first appearing in the Triassic. Today they live in the Andes mountains in South America. The tightly packed leathery leaves may live for 15 years before falling off the branch.

HORSETAILS
Horsetails date from the Devonian. Some grew as trees in the Coal Measure swamps reaching heights of 18 m (60 ft). This is the stem of a Jurassic *Equisetites*.

Leaf-bearing part of stem

Equisetites

Underground part of stem

37

Continued on next page

continued from previous page

Protected seeds

Most modern seed-producing plants have their seeds protected in a fruit (flowering plants, or angiosperms) or a cone (gymnosperms, including conifers). Angiosperms are the most successful of modern plants. There are an estimated 250,000 species as compared with 50,000 species of all other plants. Grasses, oaks, tulips, palms, potatoes, and cacti are all angiosperms. In spite of their great variety, angiosperms appear relatively late in the fossil record. The earliest examples come from the Cretaceous. The earliest conifer fossils occur earlier, in the Carboniferous.

SOFT FRUIT
All fruits contain seeds of some sort. Soft fruits decay quickly. Hard seeds are more likely to be fossilized.

Palm-like leaf

Fossil cycad

BEFORE THE FLOWERS
When angiosperms first appeared, some of the most common plants were cycads. These were palm-like gymnosperms which produced seeds in separate cone-like structures. Modern cycads still look like palms. There are nine kinds living in tropical and sub-tropical forests.

Sabal leaf

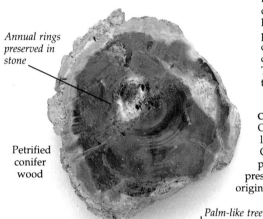

Annual rings preserved in stone

Petrified conifer wood

CYCAD COMPANION
Other gymnosperms were also living at this time, and some Cretaceous conifer wood has been petrified (turned to stone). This has preserved remarkable details of the original wood.

FOSSIL PALM
There are two main types of angiosperms - monocotyledons and dicotyledons. Monocotyledons generally have leaves with parallel veins, dicotyledons usually have net-veined leaves. Palms, like this *Sabal* from the Eocene, and grasses are monocotyledons. All other angiosperms shown are dicotyledons.

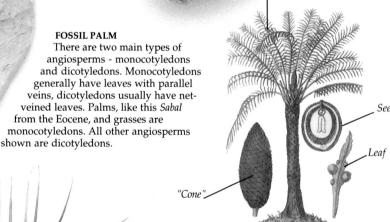

Palm-like tree

Seed

Leaf

"Cone"

Modern cycad

SPLIT IN TWO
Angiosperm leaves are relatively common and well-preserved in some fine-grained sedimentary rocks. This Miocene example of a myrtle leaf has been fractured into two parts.

Leaf of a modern palm

Fossil *Nipa* fruit

COAST GUARDS
A fruit of a modern *Nipa* tree is compared here with a smaller fossil *Nipa* fruit from the Eocene. *Nipa* is a stemless palm which grows today along tropical coastlines or rivers close to the coast. It has an important role in preventing coastal erosion.

Modern *Nipa* fruit

FLAT CHESTNUT
This is the flattened seed of a water chestnut from the Miocene.

Fossil poplar leaf

SMALL CHANGE
Fossil poplar leaves are almost identical to poplars today. This beautiful example is about 25 million years old. Modern poplar trees can grow to 40 m (130 ft) tall and each sheds a huge number of potentially fossilizable leaves during its lifetime.

Modern poplar leaves

Palliopora seeds

Juglans seeds

Mastixia seeds

Tectocarya seeds

Greatly magnified fossil pollen

FIRST POLLEN
This Cretaceous pollen grain is one of the earliest-known types of angiosperm pollen.

ANCIENT SEEDS
Angiosperm seeds are often enclosed in a fleshy fruit which animals eat – the seeds are then dispersed. Various types of fossil fruits and seeds are common from the late Cretaceous onwards. All those shown here are about 30 million years old.

GIANT CONIFER
Giant redwoods are conifers now living only in North America. Remains can be found in Jurassic and younger rocks. Conifers are gymnosperms and produce seeds inside cones. Fossils include rooted stumps and fallen trunks as well as cones and seeds.

Fossil Miocene leaves

Fossil maple leaf showing midrib and veins

LEAVES IMPRESSIONS
These Miocene leaves are beautifully preserved as impressions in a fine-grained limestone. The three-lobed leaf with midrib and delicate veins is easy to identify as that of a maple, although very little of the original plant tissue remains.

Leaves of a modern maple

Bud

BUDDING MAPLE
Buds are rarely preserved in fossil plants but, remarkably, one is attached to this flattened twig of a Miocene maple tree.

STONE RINGS
Growth rings, like those that can be seen in the wood of trees living today, show clearly in this polished section of petrified oak wood. They provide useful information about the seasonal growth of the tree, and the climate at the time the tree was living.

Growth rings

Fossil flower

PRESERVED PETALS
Although fossils of flowering plants are common, the flowers themselves are seldom found, being delicate and short lasting. Therefore, these petals of *Porana* from the Miocene are exceptional. A flower of today with similar petals is the primrose.

Modern primrose

Fossil fuels

OIL AND COAL are known as fossil fuels because they originate from ancient organisms, mainly plants. When we burn them we release the energy, in the form of heat and light, which was originally captured by the living plants during photosynthesis millions of years ago. Fossil fuels are extracted from the Earth in huge quantities. Not only are they burnt to give energy, they are also used in the manufacture of many synthetic materials.

A Coal Measure forest

Living mosses and grasses

PEAT
The plants growing on top of this peat will eventually die and add their rotting remains to the peat beneath. Dried peat is sometimes used as a fuel in household fires.

COAL PLANT
This is the impression of the bark of one of the plants which lived in the vast Coal Measure forests of the Carboniferous. About two-thirds of the world's coal supplies were formed by the plants of these forests.

Crack caused when drying

LIGNITE
The first stage of coal formation, typically dark brown in colour, may still contain some water. It crumbles easily and may crack as it dries in the air.

From plant to coal

Coal is formed after millions of years by the decay and burial of plants that usually grow in freshwater swamps. Special conditions are needed for coal to form. During the early stages of the process, oxygen must not be present so that bacterial decay of the plants can lead to the formation of peat. The peat is then buried and compressed under the weight of more sediment and rotting plants. It undergoes chemical changes resulting first in lignite, then bituminous coal, and finally, if temperatures and pressures become sufficiently high, anthracite coal.

Impression of lycopod bark

BITUMINOUS COAL
Black bituminous coal is the most common coal for household fires. The impression of a Carboniferous lycopod tree (p. 36) seen here shows the plant origin of the coal.

MODERN MINING
Most coal is extracted by deep mining. When the coal is near the surface, it is extracted by opencast working.

COAL LABOUR
Wagons full of coal were once hauled through the underground tunnels by men, women, and children. Nowadays, there are conveyor belts, or trucks pulled by engines.

Ink

Shoepolish

ALL MADE FROM COAL
Most coal is burnt to give heat in household fires, or to make steam which, in turn, is used to drive the generators in power stations producing electricity. But many everyday products used in the home and garden are also made from coal. These include coal-tar soap, ink, and shoepolish. Other products sometimes made from coal are antiseptics, drugs, dyes, detergents, perfumes, nail varnish, fertilizers, weedkillers, insecticides, nylon, and plastics.

Coal-tar soap

ANTHRACITE
Anthracite is a hard, intensely black and shiny coal. It is the best-quality coal.

OIL PLANT

This is a greatly enlarged fossil of a microscopic Eocene plant which lived in the sea. Similar planktonic plants were the originators of oil. Their fossilized remains provide important clues about rocks, useful to geologists searching for oil.

NO OIL
This core of rock, cut during drilling for geologists to examine, does not contain any oil.

OIL-BEARING
This dark piece of porous core does contain oil. Oil does not form huge underground lakes but is held as tiny droplets in the pores in the rock - rather similar to the way water is held in a sponge.

Light crude oil

Heavy crude oil

CRUDE OILS
It can be extremely difficult to get oil out of rock. Often, the presence of natural gas helps force the oil up to the surface, but sometimes pressure is too low and the oil has to be pumped up. Crude oils, oils in their natural state, vary widely. The heaviest oils, formed at relatively low temperatures, are black, thick, and waxy. The lightest oils, formed at high temperatures, are pale and thin. All crude oils must be refined before they can be used.

REFINED OIL
Oils are treated in a refinery. Refining is a very complex process and there are several different stages.

From plankton to oil

Oil and natural gas are together known as petroleum from the Latin words *petra* (rock) and *oleum* (oil). They were formed mainly by the decomposition of tiny planktonic plants which lived near the surface of the sea. When they died, their remains sank to the sea bed and were buried in mud. Over millions of years, this mud turned to rock and the organic remains formed specks of carbon-rich kerogen, an early stage of oil, and then oil. Oil is often found some distance away from where it originated. It migrates, or moves, generally upwards through porous rocks which have tiny spaces into which it can seep. If it meets an impervious layer of rock, which has no pores, the oil cannot migrate. It may therefore become trapped in what is then called a "reservoir rock".

Modern oil rig

Three cones of the bit

DRILLING FOR OIL
The most common drill bit is a tri-cone bit like this one. Bits cut through rock by being rotated at the bottom of a hollow drill pipe down which a muddy fluid is pumped. This fluid lubricates and cools the bit and carries away the fragments of rock.

An early way of drilling for oil

Polyester scarf

Fossil foraminifers

MICROSCOPIC FOSSILS
Fossils of foraminifers, microscopic animals with chalky shells, are often used by geologists to date rocks.

Sunglasses

Wax crayons

ALL MADE FROM OIL
Once in the refinery, oil is separated into different liquids, gases, and solids. These are used to make a wide range of products in addition to petrol, diesel, and lubricating oil. Many detergents, paints, plastics, and clothes are derived from petroleum chemicals. These wax crayons, sunglasses, and polyester scarf are all by-products of oil.

Out of the water

Fleshy outline of the body

COLONIZATION OF THE LAND by vertebrates, 350 million years ago, was made possible through the evolution of lungs for breathing air, and limbs for walking. Air-breathing was inherited by the first land vertebrates, amphibians, from their fish ancestors. Fishes with lungs for breathing – lungfishes (p. 35) – still exist at the present day. The Australian lungfish can gulp fresh air from the surface of drying ponds while other fishes die in the foul water. Limbs for walking developed from muscular fins similar to those seen in the living coelacanth (p. 61). Most amphibians have a larval stage (tadpole) which has to live in water and for this reason, they must return to water to lay their eggs.

CURIOUS CREATURE
This curious amphibian, *Diplocaulus*, from the Permian of Texas, U.S.A., lived in ponds and streams.

Long hind legs

FOSSIL FROG
This fossil frog is a female of a species of *Discoglossus*. It comes from the Miocene of West Germany. The specimen is unusual in showing the fleshy outline of the body and long hind legs. Frogs first appeared in the Triassic but are seldom found fossilized because their delicate bones decay very easily.

Eyes

FOSSIL TADPOLE
Even rarer than fossils of adult frogs are fossils of their tadpoles. The two eyes can be clearly seen in this Cenozoic specimen of *Pelobates*.

ETERNAL YOUTH
The axolotl is an unusual salamander from Central America. It normally remains in a "larval" stage throughout its life, using its feathery external gills to breathe underwater and not coming on to land. The name axolotl comes from an appropriate Aztec word meaning "water monster".

GOING THROUGH STAGES
Like most amphibians, frogs usually have to lay their eggs in water. These hatch into tadpoles which live in the water. As they develop, tadpoles go through different stages before they leave the water as miniature frogs. Lungs and skin replace gills as a means of breathing, fore and hind legs grow, and the tail gradually disappears.

Heavy hip bones

SURVIVING AMPHIBIAN
The early inhabitants of the land differed in many ways from the amphibians which have survived to the present day such as frogs, toads, newts, and salamanders. This is a modern natterjack toad.

Strong foot

EARLY ANCESTOR
One of the earliest known amphibians, *Ichthyostega*, is found in Devonian rocks in Greenland. It is regarded by some palaeontologists as an ancestor of all later amphibians. It was apparently able to walk on land, had lungs for breathing air, but still had a tail-fin like a fish.

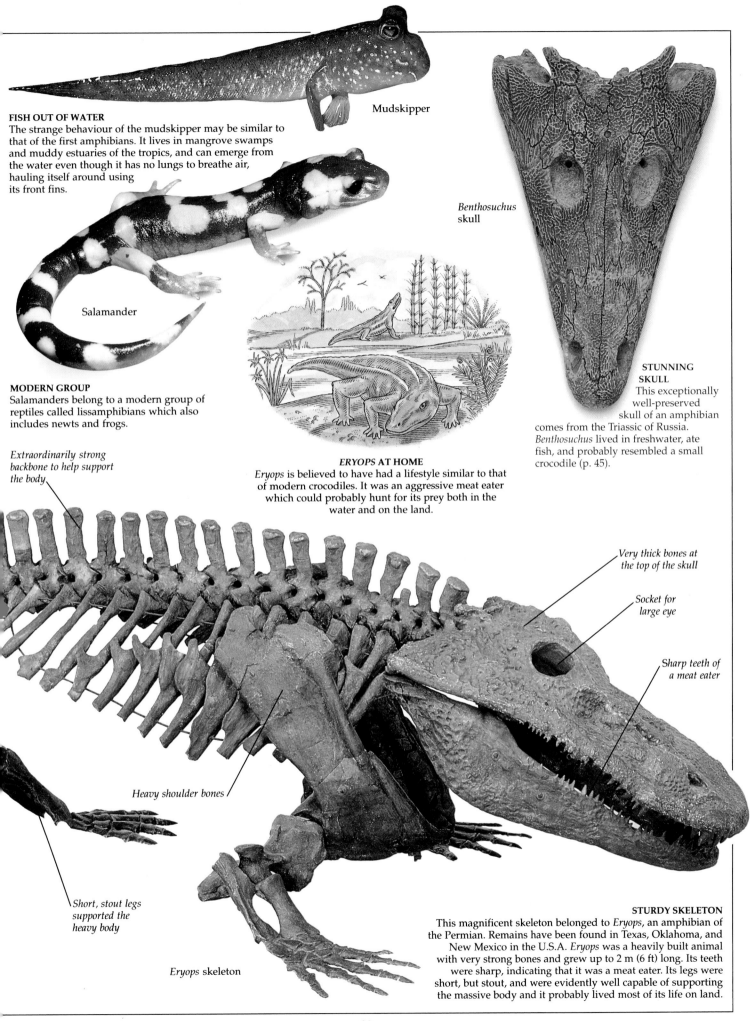

Mudskipper

FISH OUT OF WATER
The strange behaviour of the mudskipper may be similar to that of the first amphibians. It lives in mangrove swamps and muddy estuaries of the tropics, and can emerge from the water even though it has no lungs to breathe air, hauling itself around using its front fins.

Salamander

MODERN GROUP
Salamanders belong to a modern group of reptiles called lissamphibians which also includes newts and frogs.

Benthosuchus skull

STUNNING SKULL
This exceptionally well-preserved skull of an amphibian comes from the Triassic of Russia. *Benthosuchus* lived in freshwater, ate fish, and probably resembled a small crocodile (p. 45).

***ERYOPS* AT HOME**
Eryops is believed to have had a lifestyle similar to that of modern crocodiles. It was an aggressive meat eater which could probably hunt for its prey both in the water and on the land.

Extraordinarily strong backbone to help support the body

Very thick bones at the top of the skull

Socket for large eye

Sharp teeth of a meat eater

Heavy shoulder bones

Short, stout legs supported the heavy body

Eryops skeleton

STURDY SKELETON
This magnificent skeleton belonged to *Eryops*, an amphibian of the Permian. Remains have been found in Texas, Oklahoma, and New Mexico in the U.S.A. *Eryops* was a heavily built animal with very strong bones and grew up to 2 m (6 ft) long. Its teeth were sharp, indicating that it was a meat eater. Its legs were short, but stout, and were evidently well capable of supporting the massive body and it probably lived most of its life on land.

On to the land

THREE MAIN SORTS OF REPTILES live today: lizards and snakes, tortoises and turtles, and crocodiles. A fourth is represented only by the tuatara (p. 60). The number of surviving reptiles is much less than the number of extinct forms, especially those which lived in Mesozoic times such as dinosaurs (pp. 48–51), pterosaurs (p. 52), and ichthyosaurs and plesiosaurs (pp. 46–47). The first reptile fossils are found in rocks from the early Carboniferous, about 300 million years old. It is thought that these early reptiles possessed two important features, still seen in modern species, that enabled them to live away from water, unlike amphibians. They developed a special kind of egg, known as an amniote egg (below), and a scaly skin which protected their bodies against drying out.

There are over 2,000 species of snakes living today

BURIED EGGS
Oceanic turtles return to land to lay their eggs which they bury in the warm sands of tropical beaches and then return to the sea. The largest living turtle is the leatherback which may reach 2.5 m (8 ft) in length. However, the Cretaceous turtle *Archelon* grew to more than 4 m (13 ft) long!

BODY GUARD
Trionyx is a turtle from the Eocene. Only the protective carapace, or shell, is preserved here – the bones are missing. The first turtles appeared in the Triassic and probably lacked the ability of modern species to withdraw their head, limbs, and tail completely. Another difference is that they had teeth, which are replaced in modern species by a sharp horny beak for slicing vegetation or meat.

Modern ladder snake

READY FOR LAND
Turtle eggs contain liquid and have leathery shells for protection. Before birth an embryo can develop through early stages into an animal able to breathe and live on land.

LEGLESS VERTEBRATE
The earliest fossil snakes come from the late Cretaceous. Snakes have a poor fossil record but vertebrae are occasionally found. These vertebrae of *Palaeophis*, from the Palaeocene of Mali, were found separately but have been assembled to give an impression of one snake's backbone. Snakes probably evolved from a lizard-like ancestor with their limbs getting smaller and smaller and eventually disappearing altogether. This is thought to have been the result of the animal adopting a burrowing lifestyle which was later abandoned by true snakes. Two important features seen in modern snakes are the poisonous fangs, used to inject venom into prey, and the loosely connected skull bones which enable the snake to open its mouth very wide to swallow large prey.

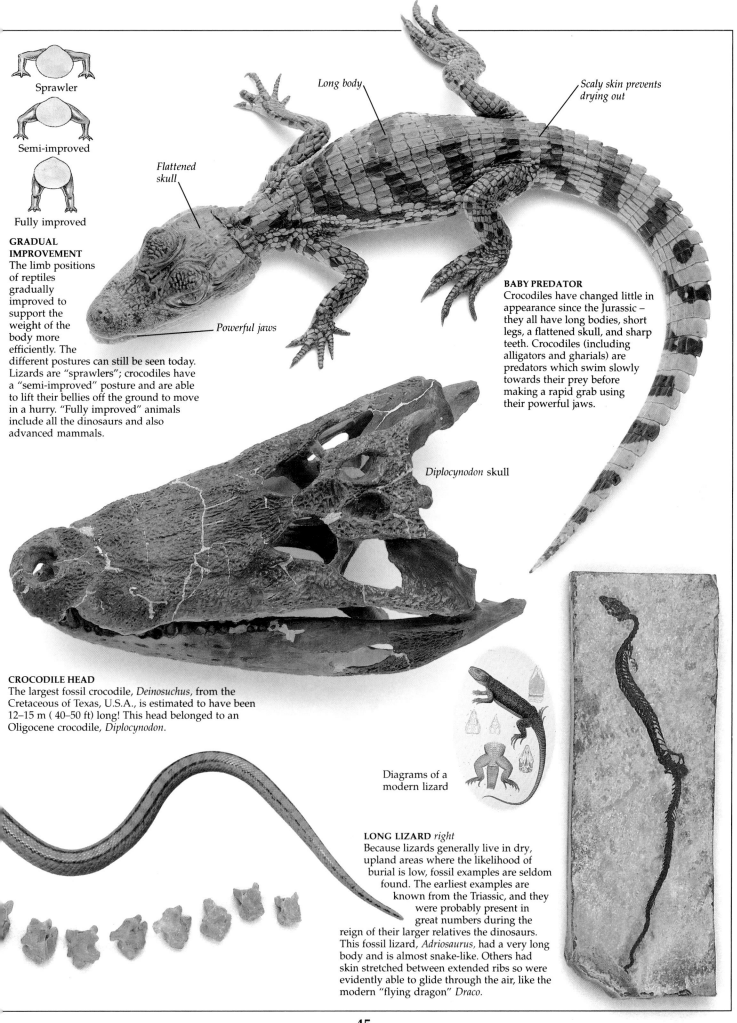

Sprawler

Semi-improved

Fully improved

GRADUAL IMPROVEMENT
The limb positions of reptiles gradually improved to support the weight of the body more efficiently. The different postures can still be seen today. Lizards are "sprawlers"; crocodiles have a "semi-improved" posture and are able to lift their bellies off the ground to move in a hurry. "Fully improved" animals include all the dinosaurs and also advanced mammals.

Flattened skull

Long body

Scaly skin prevents drying out

Powerful jaws

BABY PREDATOR
Crocodiles have changed little in appearance since the Jurassic – they all have long bodies, short legs, a flattened skull, and sharp teeth. Crocodiles (including alligators and gharials) are predators which swim slowly towards their prey before making a rapid grab using their powerful jaws.

Diplocynodon skull

CROCODILE HEAD
The largest fossil crocodile, *Deinosuchus*, from the Cretaceous of Texas, U.S.A., is estimated to have been 12–15 m (40–50 ft) long! This head belonged to an Oligocene crocodile, *Diplocynodon*.

Diagrams of a modern lizard

LONG LIZARD *right*
Because lizards generally live in dry, upland areas where the likelihood of burial is low, fossil examples are seldom found. The earliest examples are known from the Triassic, and they were probably present in great numbers during the reign of their larger relatives the dinosaurs. This fossil lizard, *Adriosaurus*, had a very long body and is almost snake-like. Others had skin stretched between extended ribs so were evidently able to glide through the air, like the modern "flying dragon" *Draco*.

Sea-dragons

DURING MESOZOIC TIMES, when dinosaurs roamed the land, the seas were inhabited by several sorts of giant reptiles popularly known as sea-dragons. The most numerous of these were the ichthyosaurs and plesiosaurs, but a third group, the mosasaurs, became common towards the end of the Mesozoic. None of these marine reptiles was really a dragon! but their remains may have contributed to the legends of the long-necked, fire-breathing monsters. Their ways of life were rather similar to modern marine mammals such as small whales, dolphins, and seals. Some were fish eaters, whereas others ate belemnites (p. 29) and other molluscs (pp. 26–29). They all breathed air and were therefore forced to surface regularly. Ichthyosaurs, plesiosaurs, and mosasaurs all became extinct, as did the dinosaurs, about 65 million years ago at the end of the Cretaceous.

MARY ANNING
Mary Anning (1799–1847) is famous for the fossils she collected close to her home in Lyme Regis on the south coast of England. The cliffs here contain abundant fossils of animals which lived in the sea in Jurassic times. Between 1810 and 1812 Mary and her brother excavated a complete ichthyosaur (at the time thought to be a crocodile) which they sold for £23, a large sum of money in those days.

A GOOD LIKENESS
The similarity in shape between modern dolphins and ichthyosaurs suggests they had a similar lifestyle.

Dorsal fin for steering

Backbone

Kink in backbone

Powerful tail for swimming

Pointed tooth

A mosasaur

Excavation of a mosasaur jaw from a chalk mine at Maastricht in the Netherlands, in the 18th century

JAW OF A GIANT LIZARD
Three pointed teeth are visible in this fragment of a mosasaur jaw from the Cretaceous. Mosasaurs were closely related to monitor lizards of today but monitor lizards live on land. Mosasaurs grew up to 9 m (30 ft) long, and were probably slow-moving predators. They existed for a relatively short time in geological history, being known only from the late Cretaceous.

Ring of bones around eye socket

Short, sharp teeth

SAMUEL CLARKE

Samuel Clarke (1815–1898) was an amateur geologist who lived near Lyme Regis. He knew the area well and directed professionals to the most likely spots for finding sea-dragons. He is holding here the skull of a plesiosaur found in 1863.

PACKED TEETH

The long jaws of most ichthyosaurs are crammed with short, sharp teeth. Ichthyosaurs had large eyes and it is thought that the ring of bones around the eye sockets improved their focusing ability. Their nostrils were far back on the top of the skull, as in modern dolphins and whales. This made it easier for the animals to breathe when they surfaced for air.

BATTLE OF THE SEA-DRAGONS

A fictitious encounter between an ichthyosaur and a long-necked plesiosaur.

Outline of soft tissue

Neck vertebrae close together

Long jaws

Eye socket

Packed teeth

STREAMLINED PREDATOR

The streamlined shape of an ichthyosaur is seen in this fine Jurassic specimen where an outline of the soft tissues has been preserved as well as the skeleton. The neck vertebrae of ichthyosaurs were close together so that the head ran smoothly into the body. This is typical of fast-swimming predators and is also seen in dolphins today. Ichthyosaurs swam by moving their powerful tails. Their backbones had a downward kink as they continued only into the lower part of the tail fin. When the first skeletons were discovered it was thought that these were broken tails. The dorsal fin and paddles were used for steering and stability. Unlike most reptiles, ichthyosaurs gave birth to live young. Some specimens have been found with young inside the body cavity of adults, and several examples are known of mothers fossilized in the act of giving birth.

Paddle for steering

PADDLE POWER

The limbs of plesiosaurs formed large paddles. Like a turtle, a plesiosaur probably flapped these up and down when swimming.

TIME OF THE ICHTHYOSAURS

Dating from the Triassic, ichthyosaurs were especially common in the Jurassic and survived into the late Cretaceous.

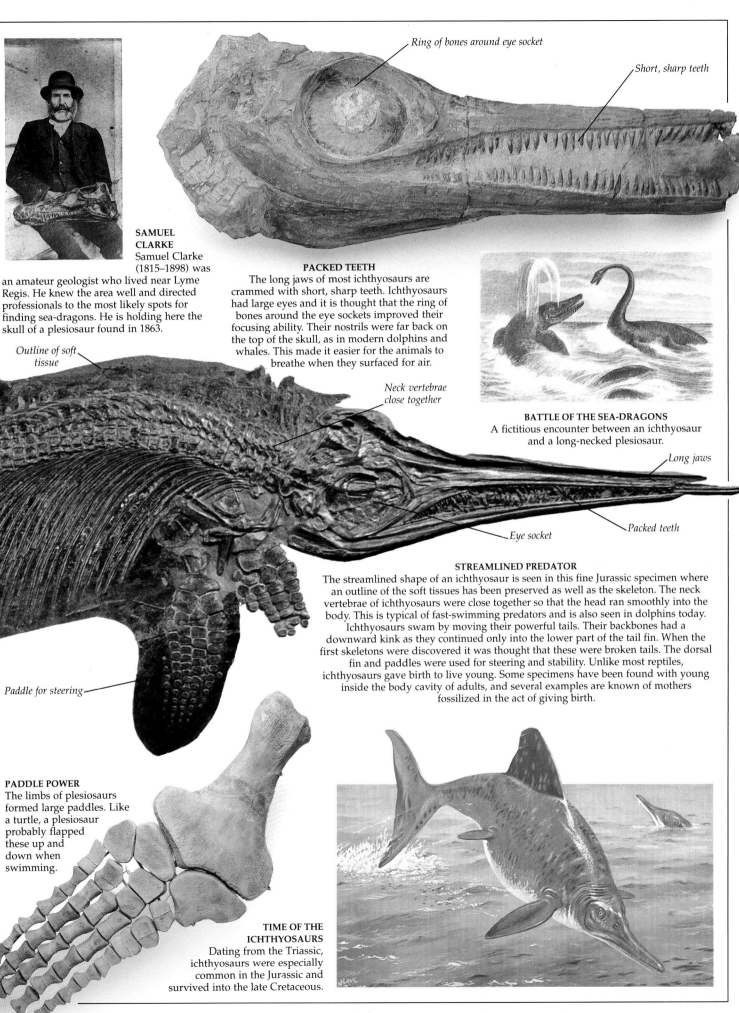

Fossil giants

Dinosaurs are probably the most impressive of all fossils. There were many different species, and their reign spanned 150 million years from the Triassic to the end of the Cretaceous. Dinosaurs were reptiles. Not all of them were huge; there were large ones and small ones. Some were plant eaters, others were meat eaters. Some had armoured plates, others had spiked or clubbed tails. The variety was enormous. We know about dinosaurs from their skeletons, and detailed restorations of them can be made from their bones (p. 14). We cannot know for certain what colour they were but can make a guess based on the colour of reptiles living today. The mysterious extinction of the dinosaurs at the end of Cretaceous times has stimulated many different theories such as a change in climate or a meteor impact. The dinosaurs did not all die out at once. By the end of the Cretaceous, they were already reduced from hundreds of species to fewer than twenty.

FOOD GRINDER
This Jurassic sauropod, *Apatosaurus*, weighed about 30 tonnes. Like all sauropods, it was a plant eater, probably using its long neck to reach leaves on trees. Its teeth were relatively small and it is thought that *Apatosaurus* swallowed stones which then acted as a mill, grinding up the food in its stomach. Modern crocodiles use stones in a similar way.

MONSTER-STALKING
Although all the giant Mesozoic reptiles became extinct long before humans appeared, some people still search for living examples of these monsters.

Edmontosaurus

PLANT EATER
One of the last-surviving dinosaurs was *Edmontosaurus*. It was a hadrosaur, or duck-bill, which grew to about 13 m (43 ft) long. Hadrosaurs were once thought to live partly in water, feeding on water plants, but land-plant fossils have been found with some skeletons, which suggests that a diet of trees and shrubs was more likely. These were dealt with by powerful teeth – about 1,000 in *Edmontosaurus*. Hadrosaurs laid their eggs in mound-shaped nests. A colony of hadrosaur nests was discovered in Montana, U.S.A. The nests were grouped closely together with young of different ages in them, indicating that the animals may have lived in herds and that the adults apparently protected their young.

Powerful teeth for crushing leaves

Skull of
Edmontosaurus

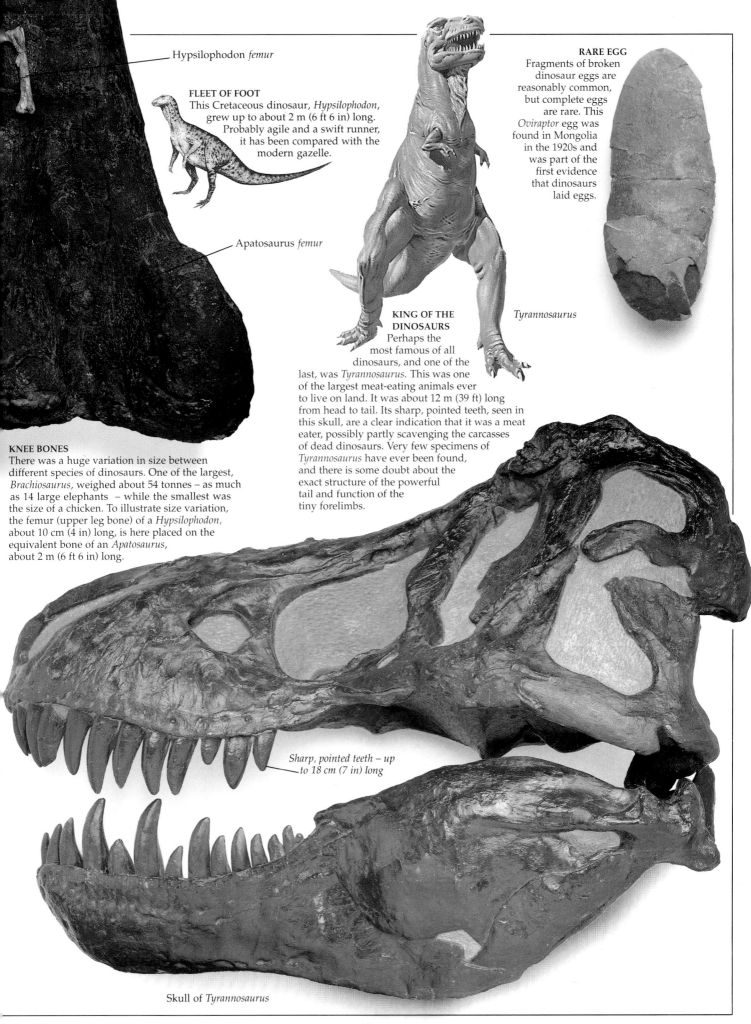

Hypsilophodon *femur*

FLEET OF FOOT
This Cretaceous dinosaur, *Hypsilophodon*,
grew up to about 2 m (6 ft 6 in) long.
Probably agile and a swift runner,
it has been compared with the
modern gazelle.

Apatosaurus *femur*

RARE EGG
Fragments of broken
dinosaur eggs are
reasonably common,
but complete eggs
are rare. This
Oviraptor egg was
found in Mongolia
in the 1920s and
was part of the
first evidence
that dinosaurs
laid eggs.

Tyrannosaurus

**KING OF THE
DINOSAURS**
Perhaps the
most famous of all
dinosaurs, and one of the
last, was *Tyrannosaurus*. This was one
of the largest meat-eating animals ever
to live on land. It was about 12 m (39 ft) long
from head to tail. Its sharp, pointed teeth, seen in
this skull, are a clear indication that it was a meat
eater, possibly partly scavenging the carcasses
of dead dinosaurs. Very few specimens of
Tyrannosaurus have ever been found,
and there is some doubt about the
exact structure of the powerful
tail and function of the
tiny forelimbs.

KNEE BONES
There was a huge variation in size between
different species of dinosaurs. One of the largest,
Brachiosaurus, weighed about 54 tonnes – as much
as 14 large elephants – while the smallest was
the size of a chicken. To illustrate size variation,
the femur (upper leg bone) of a *Hypsilophodon*,
about 10 cm (4 in) long, is here placed on the
equivalent bone of an *Apatosaurus*,
about 2 m (6 ft 6 in) long.

Sharp, pointed teeth – up
to 18 cm (7 in) long

Skull of *Tyrannosaurus*

Discovering dinosaurs

Iguanodon tooth

THE FIRST DESCRIPTIONS of the fossil bones of dinosaurs were made over 150 years ago. First some teeth, and then some bones of *Iguanodon* were found in southern England by an English doctor, Gideon Mantell, and his wife. Later, bones of the dinosaurs *Megalosaurus* and *Hylaeosaurus* were also discovered. In 1841, Sir Richard Owen, a leading British anatomist, invented the name dinosaur, which means "terrible lizard", for these early discoveries. They were followed by many more all around the world. Huge numbers of dinosaur remains were found in North America during the second half of the 19th century and into the 20th century, and other significant finds were made in Tanzania, China, Mongolia, and Argentina. Important dinosaur discoveries are still being made of species already known and of new species. Almost every new discovery adds to our knowledge of these magnificent extinct reptiles.

CLAWS DISCOVERER
Bill Walker holding the claw bone of *Baryonyx* which he discovered in 1983.

MANTELL'S TOOTH!
This is one of the original *Iguanodon* teeth which were named by Mantell in 1825.

MANTELL'S QUARRY
Mantell was a doctor of medicine and an enthusiastic collector of fossils. The *Iguanodon* teeth and bones he described came from an old quarry in the Cuckfield area of southern England. Here rocks of early Cretaceous age were dug for use as gravel.

BIG REPTILE
In 1824, William Buckland discovered some dinosaur bones in Stonesfield in Oxfordshire, England. He gave the animal the name *Megalosaurus* which means "big reptile". Later to become Dean of Westminster in London, Buckland was a teacher of geology at the University of Oxford when he described his dinosaur. This jaw bone belonged to a *Megalosaurus* and comes from the same area as Buckland's specimens.

BIG BUT NOT BIGGEST
Megalosaurus was a Jurassic meat eater related to the larger and better known *Tyrannosaurus* (p. 49).

EDWARD DRINKER COPE
Between 1870 and 1897 Cope took part in what has been described as the great dinosaur gold rush. It took place in the U.S.A., centred on the states of Montana and Wyoming. Two names are especially associated with this gold rush - Cope and Marsh. Each hired independent teams of collectors to excavate dinosaur bones in the race to be first to describe the many new species.

OTHNIEL CHARLES MARSH
In this cartoon, Marsh is depicted as a circus ringmaster leading his team of prehistoric animals. The intense rivalry between Cope and Marsh caused the two men to swap a succession of insults, and even to destroy incomplete fossils in their own quarries in order to prevent future collection by their rival!

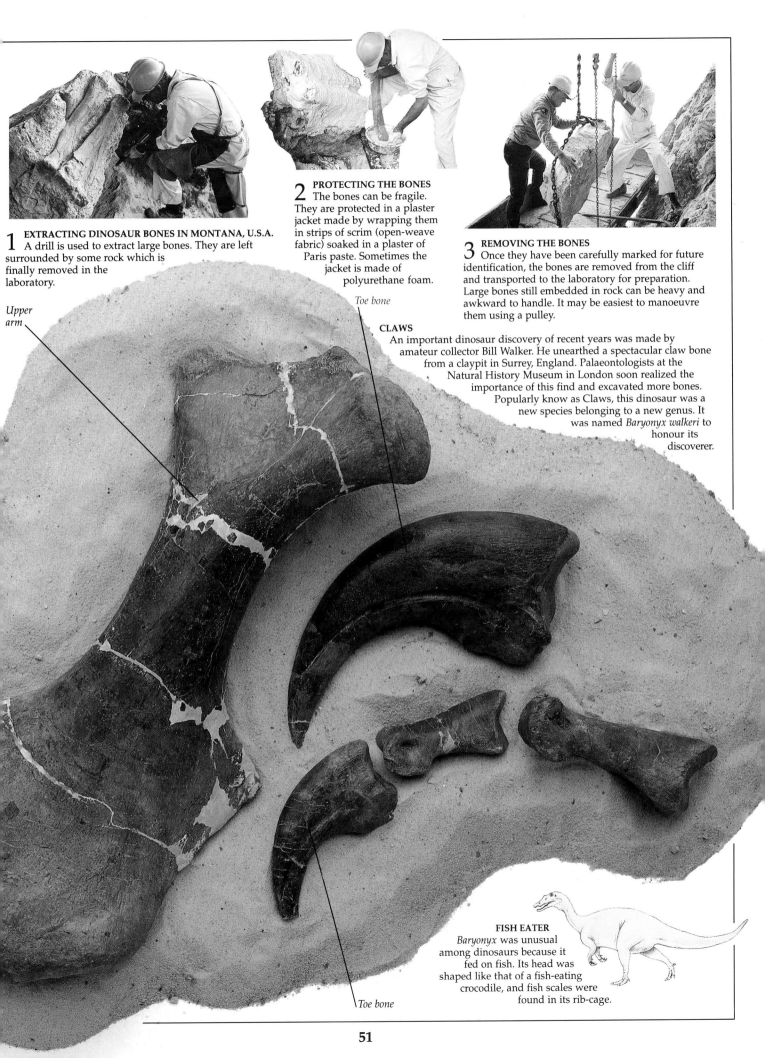

1 EXTRACTING DINOSAUR BONES IN MONTANA, U.S.A.
A drill is used to extract large bones. They are left surrounded by some rock which is finally removed in the laboratory.

2 PROTECTING THE BONES
The bones can be fragile. They are protected in a plaster jacket made by wrapping them in strips of scrim (open-weave fabric) soaked in a plaster of Paris paste. Sometimes the jacket is made of polyurethane foam.

3 REMOVING THE BONES
Once they have been carefully marked for future identification, the bones are removed from the cliff and transported to the laboratory for preparation. Large bones still embedded in rock can be heavy and awkward to handle. It may be easiest to manoeuvre them using a pulley.

CLAWS
An important dinosaur discovery of recent years was made by amateur collector Bill Walker. He unearthed a spectacular claw bone from a claypit in Surrey, England. Palaeontologists at the Natural History Museum in London soon realized the importance of this find and excavated more bones. Popularly know as Claws, this dinosaur was a new species belonging to a new genus. It was named *Baryonyx walkeri* to honour its discoverer.

Upper arm

Toe bone

Toe bone

FISH EATER
Baryonyx was unusual among dinosaurs because it fed on fish. Its head was shaped like that of a fish-eating crocodile, and fish scales were found in its rib-cage.

Winged wonders

THE FIRST ANIMALS TO FLY were insects; fossil dragonflies have been found in rocks more than 300 million years old. Flying vertebrates appeared almost 100 million years later. True flapping flight has evolved in three groups of vertebrates: the extinct pterosaurs, bats, and birds. They are not closely related, and their ability to fly has evolved independently. Pterosaurs were reptiles, related to dinosaurs (pp. 48–51), with a greatly lengthened fourth finger. This supported the fleshy membrane, a thin sheet of muscle and elastic fibres covered by skin, which was the wing. In birds, the feathered wing is supported by several fingers and the lower part of the forearm. Bats are flying mammals and have wings made of a fleshy membrane similar to that of pterosaurs but supported by four fingers. Because bones of flying vertebrates have to be light, they are fragile and are seldom fossilized.

WING SUPPORT
This is one of the long fingerbones which supported the wing of a *Pteranodon*, one of the largest-ever flying animals. The wingspan of this Cretaceous pterosaur was about 7 m (23 ft).

WELL-BALANCED
Pteranodon was a pterosaur with a bony crest on its head which counterbalanced its long toothless beak. It appears to have been a fish eater which soared over the oceans like the modern albatross.

IMAGINARY BIRD
The finding of pterosaur remains fuelled the imagination of authors of science fiction stories.

FURRY REPTILE
The small Jurassic pterosaur *Pterodactylus* had membranous wings, claws, a toothed beak, and a body covered by fine fur. Evidence for fur comes from some pterosaurs which were discovered in Kazakhstan with hair-like impressions around the body. This may indicate that pterosaurs were warm-blooded and used the fur as insulation. The tail of *Pterodactylus* was short, and it had a wingspan of only about 50 cm (20 in), but some pterosaurs, including *Rhamphorhynchus* with a wingspan of 1.5 m (5 ft), had long tails. Pterosaurs first appeared during the Triassic and became extinct at the end of the Cretaceous.

Toothed beak

Greatly lengthened fourth finger

MISTAKEN IDENTITY
This small dinosaur belongs to a group which many scientists believe were ancestors of birds. In 1973, some museum palaeontologists in Germany realized that one of their specimens, long identified as *Compsognathus*, was really an *Archaeopteryx*!

Membranous wing

Short tail

Body covered by fine fur

Claws

FLYING MAMMAL
It is easy to see the similarity between this bat and the pterosaurs. Bats date from the Eocene. Because bats often roost in caves, their fossil bones can be found in large numbers in cave deposits.

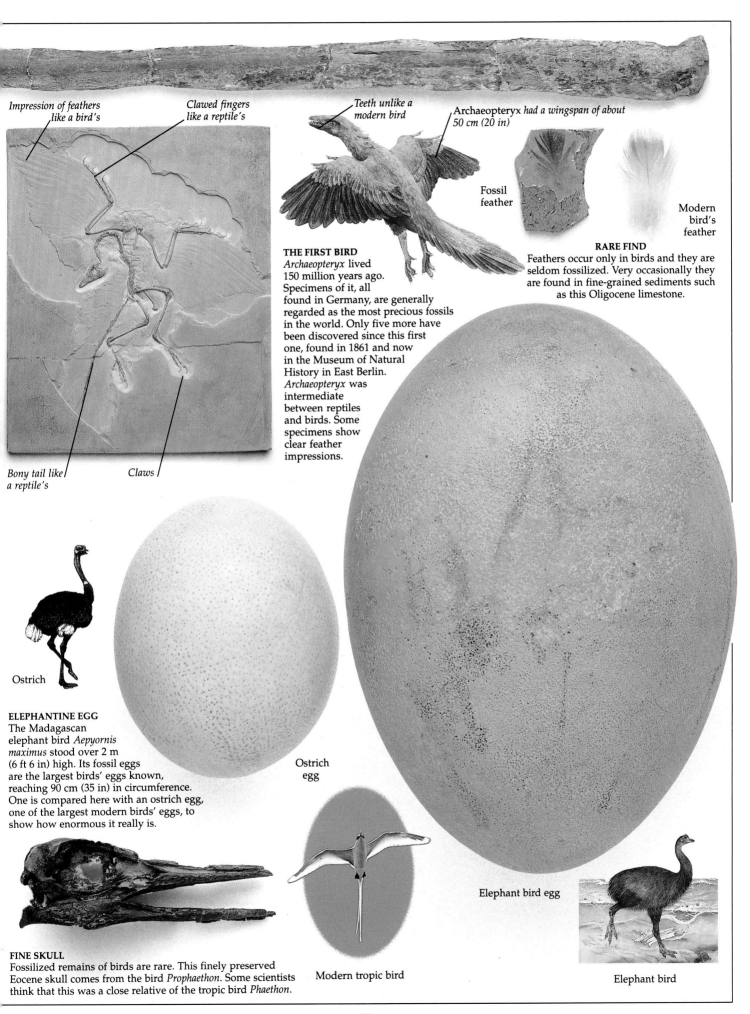

Impression of feathers like a bird's

Clawed fingers like a reptile's

Teeth unlike a modern bird

Archaeopteryx *had a wingspan of about 50 cm (20 in)*

Fossil feather

Modern bird's feather

THE FIRST BIRD
Archaeopteryx lived 150 million years ago. Specimens of it, all found in Germany, are generally regarded as the most precious fossils in the world. Only five more have been discovered since this first one, found in 1861 and now in the Museum of Natural History in East Berlin. *Archaeopteryx* was intermediate between reptiles and birds. Some specimens show clear feather impressions.

RARE FIND
Feathers occur only in birds and they are seldom fossilized. Very occasionally they are found in fine-grained sediments such as this Oligocene limestone.

Bony tail like a reptile's

Claws

Ostrich

ELEPHANTINE EGG
The Madagascan elephant bird *Aepyornis maximus* stood over 2 m (6 ft 6 in) high. Its fossil eggs are the largest birds' eggs known, reaching 90 cm (35 in) in circumference. One is compared here with an ostrich egg, one of the largest modern birds' eggs, to show how enormous it really is.

Ostrich egg

Elephant bird egg

FINE SKULL
Fossilized remains of birds are rare. This finely preserved Eocene skull comes from the bird *Prophaethon*. Some scientists think that this was a close relative of the tropic bird *Phaethon*.

Modern tropic bird

Elephant bird

53

Mammal variety

ANIMALS AS VARIED AS MICE, ELEPHANTS, kangaroos, bats, cats, whales, horses, and humans are all mammals. They are warm-blooded and produce milk to suckle their infants. Most give birth to live young, have hairy skins, complex teeth, and are highly active. A mammal whose babies develop inside the mother's womb like a cat is known as a placental mammal. The babies of marsupial mammals (pp. 56–57), such as the kangaroo, develop inside the mother's pouch after birth. The first mammals appeared at about the same time as the earliest dinosaurs, 200 million years ago. Nearly all Mesozoic mammals were small shrew-like animals, but in the Cenozoic they diversified into the many different types we are familiar with today. Complete fossil mammals are rare; many species are known only from their teeth. Nevertheless, from these it is possible to build up a picture of the variety of species and the way they lived, especially their different diets.

Chisel-like incisor teeth

Skull of *Ischyromys*

Berries

RODENTS

Rodents include rats, mice, and squirrels, and are among the most diverse of mammals. Their large chisel-like incisor teeth grow continuously during life and are used to gnaw a variety of foods. Rodents date from Palaeocene times. This example is *Ischyromys* from the famous Oligocene mammal beds of the White River Badlands in South Dakota, U.S.A.

Modern squirrel

Ants

Skull of *Orycteropus*

INSECT EATERS

Insect-eating mammals are generally small and include shrews and moles. *Orycteropus* was a Miocene aardvark, a peculiar kind of anteater. Mammals living on a diet of ants have several features in common, including a long hard palate in the roof of the mouth which helps prevent ants from entering the windpipe.

Modern aardvark

High-crowned cheek teeth

Modern camel

Skull of *Cainotherium*

ICE-AGE MAMMAL

Mammoths were elephant-like mammals adapted to life in cold climates during the Pleistocene Ice Ages. Some skeletons have been found preserved in the frozen ground of Siberia (p. 20).

PLANT EATERS

Many herbivorous mammals which feed on vegetation have cheek teeth with high crowns capable of withstanding wear caused by constant chewing. They divide into browsers, those that eat mostly leaves, and grazers, those that eat mostly grass. This skull belonged to *Cainotherium*, a rabbit-like browser whose closest, but very distant, living relative is probably a camel.

Ridges of hard enamel

GRINDING TOOTH

Mammoths were enormous and needed to eat large quantities of vegetation. Their huge high-crowned cheek teeth had ridges of hard enamel on the grinding surface. This enabled them to grind up vegetation with great efficiency.

Leaves

Skull of *Proconsul*

Blunt teeth typical of a fruit eater

FRUIT EATERS
Monkeys and apes, and humans belong to a group of mammals called the primates. Many primates are omnivores and so have a mixed diet, but some eat mostly fruit. Shown here is the skull of the Miocene ape *Proconsul*. The blunt teeth are typical of fruit eaters. As fruit is poor in protein, *Proconsul* may have supplemented its diet with leaves from the trees in which it lived.

Modern monkey

Fruit

Nuts

EOCENE LANDSCAPE
Mammals first became common in the Eocene. Many of the mammals which roamed the land belonged to groups with no living descendants.

Skull of *Hoplophoneus*

Large canine tooth

Meat

Sabretooth cat

MEAT EATERS
Carnivorous mammals which eat meat have large canine teeth. These were developed to their greatest extent in the upper jaws of the so-called sabretooths. They may have used their long teeth to stab the necks of their prey. This skull belongs to *Hoplophoneus* from the Oligocene. Alas, none of the several different sorts of sabretooth known from the fossil record has survived to the present day.

Canine tooth

Skull of *Potamotherium*

FISH EATERS
Potamotherium lived in freshwater lakes during the early Miocene and fed on fish. It was similar to a modern otter but was better adapted to life in water than otters. It may have been a forerunner of seals which first became common in the sea during the late Miocene.

Fish

Modern otters

55

A boxing kangaroo

A world apart

AUSTRALIA IS AN ISLAND CONTINENT. The geological record shows that it has been isolated for 50 million years, ever since plate movements (pp. 12–13) caused the continent to drift away from Antarctica. This is the reason why many of the native mammals in Australia are unique. Marsupials differ from other mammals in having pouches in which the young are reared for a period after birth. The fleshy pouches do not fossilize but there are features of the bones and teeth which distinguish fossils of marsupials from those of placentals (pp. 54–55). Marsupials evolved on their own, away from the placental mammals which came to dominate over them in other parts of the world. Fossils of many extinct marsupials have been found including *Diprotodon*, the centrepiece of this spread. There are still many species of pouched mammal in Australia including the kangaroo and koala. Other native mammals unique to the country include the extraordinary egg-laying monotremes – the platypus and the echidna.

Hip bone connecting the leg to the spine

TWO FRONT TEETH
This magnificent skeleton of the extinct marsupial *Diprotodon* is about 3 m (10 ft) long. Its name, meaning "two front teeth", refers to the large rodent-like incisors which were used for cropping vegetation. Note the pair of epipubic bones in the pelvic area which can be used to distinguish pouched from placental mammals. *Diprotodon* comes from Pleistocene rocks and many skeletons have been excavated from Lake Callabonna, a dried-up lake in South Australia. It is possible that *Diprotodon* survived until more recent times and was hunted by early Australians – some animals in ancient Aboriginal paintings could be *Diprotodon*.

60 million years ago

Australia

Antarctica

Epipubic bones which helped support the pouch

Tail vertebrae

45 million years ago

Australia

Antarctica

DRIFTING CONTINENTS
These two maps show the position of Australia about 60 million years ago (top) and 45 million years ago (bottom) after the split from Antarctica. The isolation of Australia prevented its colonization by placental mammals, apart from some bats and rodents. These might otherwise have replaced the native animals. This is probably what happened to the marsupials of South America, such as the extinct sabretooth *Thylacosmilus*, when placental mammals invaded South America after North and South America were joined.

GIANT WOMBAT?
Diprotodon (above) was a herbivore. It probably looked like a long-legged wombat (opposite).

Spine, the main support for the body

Blunt teeth for grinding vegetation

Rodent-like incisors for cropping vegetation

Rib cage which protected the heart and lungs

Placental mammals

Wolf

Ocelot

Ground hog

Australian marsupials

Tasmanian wolf

Native cat

Wombat

THE OUTBACK
The climate of Australia in the Pliocene became drier and grasslands spread at the expense of forests. The Australian outback is now dry and inhospitable for humans. However, many native species of mammals thrive there, and parts of Australia may have been equally inhospitable when *Diprotodon* lived.

Procoptodon

Young kangaroo in the pouch

Modern kangaroo

ALIKE BUT DIFFERENT
A remarkable feature of mammal evolution is that for many placental mammals there is an equivalent pouched mammal in Australia. This is called parallel evolution and it happened because the animals adapted to similar ways of life. The placental wolf which lives on all other continents is matched in Australia by the Tasmanian wolf. Sadly this animal became extinct about 70 years ago.

A FAKE?
When the remains of a platypus were first brought to London in the 18th century, they were dismissed as a fake! The platypus lives in fresh-water, has fur, webbed feet, and a beak. It lays eggs but suckles its young! It may show an early stage in mammal development.

GIANT KANGAROO
Large grazing kangaroos did not become common until the Pliocene, although the ancestors of modern kangaroos can be traced back to the Miocene. A kangaroo of the Pleistocene, *Procoptodon*, was 3 m (10 ft) tall! A species of modern kangaroo reaches about 2 m (6–7 ft) when extended to its full height.

Human fossils

Fossils of people (hominids) are rare and fragmentary, but have been found in increasing numbers during the past few years. They tell us a great deal about the origin and development of modern people. The story begins with the ape-like *Ardipithecus* and *Australopithecus* and ends with *Homo sapiens*. The nearest living relatives of humans are the African Great Apes (chimpanzees and gorillas) but there are many differences between us and them. These include a larger brain in humans and the ability to walk on two legs rather than four legs. Study of fossil hominids shows how these differences developed through geological time. Typical human features first appeared in *Australopithecus*, distinguishing them from their even more ape-like ancestors.

SHOT BY AN ALIEN?
"Bullet hole"
This skull from Broken Hill, Zambia belongs to an early form of our own species, *Homo sapiens*. It is famous for its bad teeth and the hole in one side. An imaginative writer interpreted this as a hole made by a bullet shot by a visitor from another planet 120,000 years ago! In fact it is a partly healed abscess.

Adult's footprint
Child's footprint

FIRST STEPS
At some stage in human evolution, bipedalism (standing upright and walking on two legs) developed. These footprints from Tanzania were made by two-footed hominids 3.6 million years ago. They were probably two adults and a child *Australopithecus* who walked across a surface of damp volcanic ash. The ash hardened and was buried beneath more ash and sediment. The fossil footprints were discovered by a team led by Mary Leakey in 1977. They prove that a species of primate walked on two feet at least 3.6 million years ago. This ties in with evidence from fossil bones that *Australopithecus* walked on two legs.

Chimpanzee skull

Human skull

COMPARING FEATURES
These skulls of a modern human and an ape – a chimpanzee – look very similar, but careful comparison shows some of the differences. Humans have much larger brains than chimps. The average volume of a human's brain is 1,400 cc whereas a chimp's brain is about 400 cc. This is reflected in the domed human cranium, necessary to house the large brain, compared with the low chimp cranium. Another obvious difference is the flatter muzzle of the human. The teeth are also different. For example, a chimp cannot move its jaws from side to side so much when it is chewing, as its canine teeth overlap.

Carved reindeer

ARTISTIC BEGINNINGS
This sculpted antler is over 12,000 years old and shows a male reindeer following a female reindeer. It was probably carved using simple flint tools and reveals a high quality of craftsmanship. Such art forms show the development of the cultural activities (art, literature, music etc) which are unique to humans.

Using a stone to chip off flakes

THE OLDEST TOOLS
The human being is often described as the toolmaker. This pebble tool is one of the oldest recognizable stone tools, thought to have been made by *Homo habilis* ("handy man") almost 2 million years ago. The flint handaxe is about 200,000 years old. Both tools were made by chipping off flakes to sharpen them.

Pebble tool

Flint handaxe

SOUTHERN APE
Several sorts of *Australopithecus* ("southern ape") lived in Africa between about 5 and 1.5 million years ago. Certain species were heavily built and had bony crests on their skulls. Others were lightly built, like this example from South Africa. It is possible that these forms are direct ancestors of modern humans.

LOUIS LEAKEY
The oldest hominids have been found in South and East Africa. Among the palaeontologists responsible for their discovery have been the Leakey family – the late Louis Leakey, his wife Mary, and son Richard. Louis, pictured here, is known especially for his finds of *Australopithecus* at Olduvai Gorge in Tanzania.

LUCY
This is the skeleton of an adult female *Australopithecus*. It was discovered in 1974 and named after the Beatles' song "Lucy in the sky with diamonds"

UPRIGHT MAN
Homo erectus ("upright man") has been found not only in Africa but also in South East Asia. They lived between about 1.6 million and 500,000 years ago. The size of the cranium indicates a brain size of about 1,000 cc, larger than *Australopithecus* but smaller than modern humans. *Homo erectus* used fire. An example from China – Peking Man – was found in a cave deposit with a fossilized hearth, used either for cooking or providing heat and light.

Carved animal head

Harpoon

ROCK PAINTING
These paintings of animals were done by early people living in what is now Algeria.

Sickle

Arrowheads

Sharp flint pieces

HUNTING TOOLS
These 4,000-year-old arrowheads are made of flint, a rock favoured by early people because of the ease with which flakes could be struck off to shape different tools. The 10,000-year-old sickle is made of goat horn with sharp pieces of flint embedded to form a cutting edge. The barbed harpoon was carved from an antler.

ICE-AGE RELATIVE
Neanderthals lived in Europe and western Asia before and during the last Ice Age, between 100,000 and 35,000 years ago. They were given the name because the first specimen to be described was found in a cave in the Neander valley, Germany. They used to be thought of as a sub-species of *Homo sapiens* ("thinking man"); today they are classed as a species alone, *Homo neanderthalensis*. The brutish cave-man image often given to Neanderthals is incorrect. On average, their brains were larger than our own. They were also shorter, stocky, and relatively hairy – well adapted to life in cold climates.

Living fossils

F<small>OSSILS SHOW US</small> that since life on Earth began, animals and plants have changed enormously. Some have changed so much that modern species are very different from their fossil ancestors. At the other extreme, there are animals and plants living today that are almost identical with fossils millions of years old. The most striking examples of these "living fossils" are those animals and plants which are rare nowadays, especially those like the coelacanth and slit shells, which were known as fossils before they were discovered to be still living. Among plant species which have survived up to the present day are the horsetail (pp. 36–37) from the Devonian, the monkey-puzzle tree (pp. 36–37) and the *Ginkgo* from the Triassic, and the magnolia, one of the earliest true flowering plants, from the Cretaceous.

LAST SURVIVOR
The tuatara is the only living survivor of a group of reptiles which were abundant during Triassic times. It looks like a lizard but its skull has a different bone structure. The tuatara lives only on a few islands off New Zealand.

Fossil horseshoe crab

FALSE CRABS
These are not true crabs but are related to spiders and scorpions. The modern horseshoe crab *Limulus* lives close to the shoreline in the Far East and in the Atlantic Ocean off North America. It is very similar to the fossil *Mesolimulus,* an animal that lived in the sea about 150 million years ago. Other fossil horseshoe crabs include species which lived in freshwater swamps 300 million years ago.

Modern horseshoe crab

ANCIENT INSECT
Still common today, cockroaches, together with dragonflies, are among the oldest of all insects and range back to the Carboniferous. Some fossil cockroaches closely resemble modern species.

Modern cockroaches

Fossil cockroach

Ginkgo *leaf*

Fan-shaped leaves

LONE RANGER
Ginkgos first appeared in the Triassic and were much more widespread in the geological past than they are today. Only a single species, *Ginkgo biloba,* lives today. Better known as the maidenhair tree, it grows naturally in the forests of western China but can also be seen in botanic gardens around the world. The characteristic fan-shaped leaves are easily recognizable when fossilized, as in this Jurassic example.

Fossil *Ginkgo*

Modern *Ginkgo* branch

ANCIENT MAMMAL
Didelphids, which include the opossums, are pouched mammals (pp. 56–57) from the Americas. Among mammals, didelphids are very old. They are first recorded in the late Cretaceous of North America. Modern opossums have many features typical of the related primitive didelphids of Cretaceous age, although they do have some significant differences.

Fossil slit shell

Modern slit shell

Modern Virginia opossum

Variety of teeth indicating a mixed diet

Fossil skull of a didelphid

BACK TO LIFE
Snails belonging to *Pleurotomaria*, the slit shells, are rare today. Living examples were first discovered in 1856 on rocky areas of the sea bed at depths greater that 200 m (650 ft). Almost identical shells had long been known as fossils. *Pleurotomaria* itself ranges back to the Jurassic, and the group in which it is classified goes back 500 million years to the Cambrian.

Slit in shell

Three-lobed tail

Fossil coelacanth

Wedgwood plate commemorating the catching of a live coelacanth

Commemorative stamps from the Comoro Islands

PRESUMED DEAD
Undoubtedly, the most famous of all living fossils is the coelacanth. Coelacanths have a distinctive three-lobed tail and fins with arm-like bases. They range back to the Devonian. It was thought that coelacanths had become extinct in Cretaceous times. Then, in December 1938, a living one was caught by a fisherman off the South African coast, causing a major stir in scientific circles. Further specimens have since been caught. Some have been photographed alive in water 60–400 m (200–1,310 ft) deep off the Comoro Islands, north-east of the island of Madagascar. Then, in 1998, a new species of coelacanth was found off the Indonesian coast, more than 9,000 km (5,600 miles) away.

WANTED!
The first modern coelacanth was identified in 1938 by Professor Smith, an ichthyologist in South Africa. He offered a reward of £100 to anyone who found a second one. He had to wait until 1952 before he had one in his possession.

Modern coelacanth

Fossil hunting

To find the fossil remains of a creature which lived millions of years ago is a thrilling experience. Fossil collecting is a hobby which can be enjoyed by anyone using the most basic of tools. Sea cliffs, quarries, and other exposures of rock all over the world provide productive places for fossil collectors but safety must always be borne in mind. It may often be necessary to get permission to collect from land owners, and regard must be paid to conservation - fossil localities can easily be ruined by over collecting.

An historic find?

CHISELS
A hammer and chisel are valuable aids when extracting fossils from their matrix (the piece of surrounding rock).

Hammer for use with a chisel

Standard geological hammer

FIELD NOTEBOOK
The type of rock formation and locality of finds should be recorded in a field notebook.

HAMMERS
A geological hammer can be used to break up rocks.

TROWELS
Fossils in soft sediment, especially sand, may be removed using a trowel.

GEOLOGICAL MAP
Geological maps are useful for locating promising places to collect fossils, as they help in identifying the age, location, and name of rock formations.

HAND LENS
A pocket hand lens with a magnification of 10 to 20 times is valuable for examining fossils in the field.

BRUSHES
Brushes can be used for brushing away sediment during excavation of fossils from soft rocks.

Safety helmet

Sieve for separating out small fossils

Bivalve

Brachiopod

IN THE FIELD
This boy should be wearing a helmet when hammering fossils out of the rock. Great care should be taken when fossil collecting. A safety helmet is a must, especially when working beneath unstable rock faces. It is often easier to collect from rocks that have already weathered loose.

DRAWER OF SPECIMENS
After cleaning with water, fossils should be stored carefully. Shallow cardboard trays are convenient for holding fossils, together with their labels. The more care that is taken over labelling a collection, the more interesting and worthwhile it will be.

Echinoid

Coral

Echinoid

Ammonite

MAGNIFYING GLASS
A large magnifying glass or a binocular microscope is invaluable for close study.

Brushes and dental picks for fossil preparation

BRACHIOPOD
Sphaeroidothyris
sphaeroidalis
Jurassic. Bajocian
Upper Inferior Oolite
East Cliff, Burton
Bradstock, Dorset,
England

LABELS
It is important to label specimens fully. Apart from the names of the fossils, details should be given of rock formation and the place where they were found. Fossils can also be numbered for future identification using sticky labels.

MICROSCOPE SLIDES
Small fossils can be kept in wooden or cardboard cavity slides, so they can be looked at under a microscope. They should be stuck down with a non-toxic, water-soluble glue or secured beneath a transparent cover glass.

Canvas bag for larger fossils

ILLUSTRATED RECORD
It is rewarding to keep a record of a collection with drawings and descriptions. These beautiful books record details of fossils collected over 100 years ago.

Plastic pots for collecting small fossils

Goggles

Did you know?

AMAZING FACTS

Dromaeosaur fossil

In the 1990s, palaeontologists began to dig up fossils of feathered dinosaurs in China – the best evidence yet that the dinosaurs may have evolved into birds. Dromaeosaurs were small, fast-moving meat-eaters that had downy fluff and primitive feathers.

The first fossils of the arthropod *Anomalocaris* were limbs, jaws, or other body parts. No one thought they belonged to one animal. The huge front limbs were thought to be tails from an extinct shrimp. It was only when a complete fossil was found that scientists could picture this strange beast at last.

Anomodonts are the most primitive beasts with mammal characteristics that we know. The 260-million-year-old skull of one was found in South Africa in 1999. About the size of sheep, anomodonts were plant-eaters that lived long before the dinosaurs. They had some reptilian characteristics, and some mammalian.

Fossils of an early whale, *Ambulocetus*, show that it was about 3 m (10 ft) long and looked like a big, furry crocodile! Although it had the teeth and skull of a whale and was an excellent swimmer, it also had legs for walking on land. Its name means "walking whale".

At Holzmaden, Germany, there are fossil specimens of thousands of Jurassic marine creatures. One of the most amazing is an ichthyosaur, fossilized in the act of giving birth.

Opalized brachiopod

Australia has large opal deposits that formed in the early Cretaceous Period. During mining for opal gems, beautiful specimens of opalized shellfish have been found, especially brachiopods. However, one of the finest opal fossils is "Eric", a complete pliosaur skeleton. Pliosaurs were marine reptiles that lived at the time of the dinosaurs.

Fossilized insect and spider in amber

In the *Jurassic Park* films, DNA from the bodies of insects fossilized in amber was used to reconstruct whole herds of dinosaurs. Scientists have extracted DNA in this way, but only fragments of it – not enough to rebuild prehistoric animals.

The first complete Pleistocene animal was excavated in 1999 by French palaeontologist Bernard Buigues. The Siberian woolly mammoth had lain frozen for over 20,000 years. It was named "Jarkov", after the family of reindeer herders who first discovered it.

In the 1990s, palaeontologists found remains of the earliest-known primate: a jawbone, and an anklebone the length of a grain of rice. Nicknamed the "Dawn Monkey", *Eosimias* was a mouse-sized primate that lived 40 to 45 million years ago in what is now China.

"Eric", the opalized pliosaur

Record Breakers

EARLIEST FOSSIL EMBRYO
The earliest known fossilized animal embryo dates back around 670 million years. It was found in Guizhou province, China.

OLDEST FOSSIL FLOWER
A 125-million-year-old flowering plant, named *Archaefructus liaoningensis*, was found in Liaoning province, China, in 1998.

LARGEST-EVER LAND MAMMAL
An 83 cm (2 ft 9 in)-long skull fossil found in Mongolia belonged to *Andrewsarchus*, an Eocene carnivore. The entire animal could have been 6 m (19 ft) long and weighed a tonne.

OLDEST FOSSIL FISH
Two fish, *Haikouichthys ercaicunensis* and *Myllokunmingia fengjiaoa*, were found in rocks from 530 million years ago in Yunnan, China.

OLDEST FOSSIL MOSS
The oldest moss fossil is 354 million years old. The moss, *Hepaticites oishii*, was discovered in Yokomichi, Japan, in 1973.

QUESTIONS AND ANSWERS

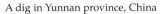

Pederpes finneyae

Q Where are the oldest fossils on Earth?

A British Columbia's Burgess Shale used to be the best site for Cambrian fossils, but now older finds are coming out of a series of sites near Kunming, in the province of Yunnan, southwest China. Preserved in rock known as the Maotianshan shales, they include the earliest examples of fish yet discovered. Thousands of near-perfect soft-bodied fossils have been found. Collectively, they are known as the "Chengjiang fauna" after a village near the sites.

Q Where in the world is the Petrified Forest?

A The Petrified Forest is a collection of fossilized logs and tree trunks scattered across an area of national park in the Arizona desert. They date back nearly 220 million years. As well as plants, there are also some amazing animal finds. These include around 40 fossilized bee nests, the earliest ever found, and lots of bone fragments from vertebrates including dinosaurs, pterosaurs, fish, primitive reptiles, and amphibians such as metoposaurs.

Fossilized sections of tree trunk in the Petrified Forest, Arizona

Q Which animal was first to walk on land?

A The earliest fossil evidence is the skeleton of a 1 m (3 ft)-long amphibian, *Pederpes finneyae*, that lived 345 million years ago. All the earlier feet fossils that have been found were designed to point back, and would have been used for swimming. *Pederpes'* ankle joints were evolved to take steps forwards. *Pederpes* probably spent some time on land, and some in the water. It lived in swamps in what is now Scotland.

Q Where did reptiles turn into mammals?

A Fossil hunters working in the Karoo Basin, South Africa, have found plenty of evidence of various "mammal-like" reptiles, called therapsids. These include the hippopotamus-like *Lystrosaurus*, the sabre-toothed predator, *Lycaenops*, and cat-sized *Thrinaxodon*. All of these creatures had characteristics of reptiles, but their teeth were more like those of mammals. This is exciting for scientists. By examining the therapsid fossils, they can start to understand the evolutionary changes that led to the first true mammals.

A dig in Yunnan province, China

Q Which American river is stocked full of fossilized fish?

A The world's richest fish fossil site is the Green River Formation at Fossil Butte National Monument, Wyoming, USA, which covers an area of 64,750 sq km (25,000 sq miles). The fossils date back some 55 million years, to the Eocene Epoch, when there was a series of large inland lakes on the site. The dead animals and plants that sank to the bottom of these lakes have been exquisitely preserved. Thousands of fish specimens have been found, from at least 20 different genera, including stingrays, catfish, herring, and trout. There are also fossils of turtles, birds, mammals, and crocodiles.

Diplomystus denatus, or herring, from the Green River Formation

Q Which are the oldest human fossils?

A In July 2001, scientists in Ethiopia announced the oldest known traces of human life. Over the previous four years, they had discovered fossils belonging to around five specimens of *Ardipithecus ramidus*, a hominid that lived between 5.2 and 5.8 million years ago. These included a jawbone, arm, hand, collar bones, toe bone, and teeth. Just a few months earlier, French scientists announced the discovery of a six-million-year-old creature, *Orrorin tugenensis*, in Kenya. This could be an even earlier human ancestor than *Ardipithecus*, but there is not yet enough evidence to classify it as a hominid.

Identifying fossils

Fossils can be split into three groups: plants, and animals with or without backbones. There are also trace fossils, such as animal tracks and coprolites. In each group, the fossil record is vast. If you ever have trouble identifying a fossil find, see if staff at a local museum can help.

FAKE FLOWER
This may look like a flower, but scientists think it was a very primitive animal, not a plant. It lived on the Precambrian seabed and was found in the fossil-rich rocks of the Ediacara Hills, Australia.

FOSSIL ID
This page is from a book that identifies invertebrate fossil finds.

PLANT FOSSILS

TREE TRUNK
Tree trunks withstand the fossilization process well. Whole forests of preserved trunks have been found, with the growth rings visible and intact.

SEQUOIA CONE
The ironstone fossil above is a pine cone from a redwood tree called a sequoia. The oldest sequoia fossils date to Jurassic times – and the trees are still around today.

CLUBMOSS
The clubmoss fossil here is *Archaeosigillaria*, which grew in the Carboniferous Period. At that time, clubmosses grew as tall as trees; today's few species are small plants.

FERN
This fern leaf was found in Hermit shale in the southwestern United States. Shales and mudstones are some of the best places to find fossils of soft plant parts.

ANIMAL FOSSILS: VERTEBRATES

BIRD
One of the world's most famous fossils, this is *Archaeopteryx*, the oldest known bird. Bavarian limestone preserved the fine imprints of its feathers and claws.

REPTILE
This skeleton is of *Pachypleurosaurus*, a reptile that lived in what is now Europe in the Middle Triassic Period. It measured around 120 cm (47 in) long.

MAMMAL
This fossil of *Macrocranion*, an Eocene hedgehog, was found at Grube Messel, Germany. The shale preserved mammals' soft body parts, as well as their skeletons.

FISH
This freshwater perch, *Priscacara*, was discovered in the fossil-rich Green River Formation, in the United States. It dates to the Middle Eocene Epoch.

TEETH
The vertebrate fossils that amateur hunters are most likely to find are teeth. Sharks, in particular, shed many teeth over a lifetime.

ANIMAL FOSSILS: INVERTEBRATES

BELEMNITE
Belemnites were molluscs related to modern-day squid and octopus. After fossilization, all that is left is the animal's inside shell, or guard.

TRILOBITE
Encrinurus, fossilized here in limestone, lived in shallow seas in the Silurian Period. Its distinctive head shield has earned it the nickname "strawberry-headed trilobite".

CRINOID (SEA-LILY)
Crinoids were common in the Palaeozoic seas. This one is *Cupressocrinites*, found in Germany. Its petal-like arms would have filtered food from the sea water.

BRACHIOPOD
About 2 cm (0.75 in) long, this brachiopod is *Goniorhynchia*, which lived in the Middle Jurassic Period. It was found in the UK, in a layer of forest marble.

AMMONITE
Gunnarites is a Late Cretaceous ammonite with a very distinctive shell. On this grey sandstone fossil, a tiny fragment of the original shell can still be seen, top left.

FORAMINIFERAN (MICROFOSSIL)
This highly-magnified image shows the fossilized test of *Elphidium*. This single-celled protozoa is tiny – about the size of a full stop.

BIVALVE
Around 7 cm (2.75 in) long, this Jurassic oyster would have cemented itself to a rock on the seabed. Called *Gryphaea*, its popular name is the Devil's toenail.

CORAL
Colpophyllia is often called "brain coral", because of the distinctive shape formed by the colony. This fossil, found in Italy, dates to the Late Oligocene Epoch.

GASTROPOD
This snail is *Pleurotomaria*, or slit shell. It has distinctive, nobbly riblets on the shoulders of the whorls. A living relative is pictured on page 61.

SPONGE
This Early Cretaceous sponge, *Raphidonema farringdonense*, is about 8 cm (3.25 in) high. It was common in warm, shallow seas in what is now Oxfordshire, England.

GRAPTOLITE
These are *Rhabdinopora*, the earliest graptolite plankton. Graptolite fossils show not one animal, but a colony of creatures that floated on the surface of the sea.

ECHINOID (SEA-URCHIN)
This extinct urchin, *Phymosoma*, lived on the sea floor in the Late Cretaceous Period. Its test and its many spines have been fossilized in chalk.

Find out more

THERE ARE SO MANY WAYS that you can find out more about fossils. Go to visit local or national museums and you will see some spectacular collections. You could look out for television programmes about fossil hunters and their exciting new finds. Visit a library or fossil websites to read up more on the subject. You could also become a fossil hunter. To do this safely, it is a good idea to join a local club, if there is one in your area. You will be glad of the guidance and expertise of the club leader. Fossil collecting is great fun, and you will soon build up your own collection to display.

PALAEONTOLOGISTS IN THE LAB
At this French laboratory, experts are carefully removing fossilized bones from a plaster cast. The plaster was set around the fossils at the place they were discovered to protect them from damage during transportation. Casts are also taken of precious, fragile fossils, for displaying. Many of the fossils on show in museums are casts.

AMATEUR FOSSIL HUNTER
It takes a great deal of patience to be a fossil hunter. Quite often, you might come home empty-handed, so it is important to enjoy the quest for its own sake. This fossil hunter in Florida is sifting through shingle, a method suitable only for certain beaches.

JET NECKLACE
See how many "fossils" you can spot in a day. Amber and jet are really just fossilized plant matter. Think about fossil fuels, too, such as coal and oil, and their many by-products.

PALAEONTOLOGIST AT WORK
Dinosaur National Monument, Colorado, is a protected site. Its fossilized dinosaur bones are exposed or dug out by professionals who will not damage them. If you want a career as a palaeontologist, aim for a good science degree and try to gather lots of experience on organized digs.

USEFUL WEBSITES

- The Earthlab datasite, with searchable information on UK fossils, rocks, and minerals
  www.nhm.ac.uk/museum/earthlab
- Guide to fossil collecting for children, from Kids' Ark
  web.ukonline.co.uk/conker/fossils
- From Bristol University: the "fun stuff" section includes files on palaeontology and an excellent dinosaur database
  palaeo.gly.bris.ac.uk
- Website for America's National Museum of Natural History
  www.mnh.si.edu
- Links to natural history museums around the world
  www.ucmp.berkeley.edu/subway/nathistmus.html

UNDER THE MICROSCOPE
At Earthlab in the Natural History Museum, London, visitors can handle real specimens and examine them under a microscope. There are experts on hand to answer questions, and to help visitors identify fossils they have found. The inner gallery also has a useful library of reference material.

THE CAMBRIDGE MUSEUM
Founded in 1814, the University Museum of Zoology in Cambridge, England, houses a superb collection of fossils. It includes fish from Canada and Scotland, mammals from North America, and reptiles from Africa. The permanent display aims to show one example of every animal – living or extinct – using fossils and stuffed specimens.

DINOSAUR MUSEUM
Europe's first museum dedicated solely to dinosaurs opened at Espéraza in southern France in 1992. Many of its display items are fossils dug from Late Cretaceous rock deposits nearby. As well as bones, the collection includes eggs, like those of the titanosaur above, and casts of fossilized footprints.

Places to visit

AMERICAN MUSEUM OF NATURAL HISTORY, NEW YORK, USA
Home to the world's largest collection of vertebrate fossils, 600 of which are on view. Highlights include:
• *Buettneria*, an early four-limbed animal
• *Pteranodon* fossil
• New reconstructions of *T-rex* and *Apatosaurus*

MUSEUM NATIONAL D'HISTOIRE NATURELLE, PARIS, FRANCE
A comprehensive natural history museum. Its attractions include:
• Gallery of specimens that chart the evolution of the vertebrate skeleton
• The world's oldest fossilized insects
• Excellent collection of plant fossils

THE NATURAL HISTORY MUSEUM, LONDON, UK
This museum has a vast collection of fossils, including exciting dinosaur exhibits. Attractions to look out for include:
• Huge *Diplodocus* reconstruction
• Earthlab, and its geology database

NATIONAL MUSEUM OF NATURAL HISTORY, WASHINGTON, USA
Part of the Smithsonian, this museum has the world's biggest collection of Burgess Shale fauna, as well as:
• Forty dinosaurs on display
• A collection of over 200,000 foraminifera

THE NATURAL HISTORY MUSEUM, PARIS
The entomology gallery in France's Natural History Museum has some of the oldest fossilized insects on Earth. There is also a palaeobotany department, dedicated to plant fossils, and a gallery of evolution, with many fossil skeletons and casts.

Glossary

Anthracite

Devonian fish

AMBER Fossilized resin of an ancient conifer.

AMMONITE An extinct cephalopod with a shell, common in the Mesozoic.

AMPHIBIAN A cold-blooded, slimy-skinned animal, adapted to life on land and in water.

ANATOMIST Someone who studies the structure of animals.

ANGIOSPERM A flowering plant that protects its seeds inside a fruit.

ANTHRACITE Hard, shiny, jet-black coal.

ARTHROPOD An animal with jointed legs, a segmented body, and an exoskeleton, for example a trilobite.

BACTERIUM One of the simplest living organisms.

BELEMNITE Extinct cephalopod related to the modern-day squid.

BIVALVE An animal with two similar shells, such as a cockle.

BRACHIOPOD An animal with two shells, one slightly larger than the other.

BYSSAL THREAD One of the stringlike attachments that fix a bivalve to the rocks.

CAMBRIAN The geological period that lasted from 545 to 495 mya.

CARBONIFEROUS The geological period that lasted from 354 to 290 mya.

CARNIVORE An animal from the *Carnivora* group.

CENOZOIC Our present geological era, which began 65 mya – the age of mammals.

CEPHALOPOD A mollusc with tentacles.

CLIMATE The average weather of a place over a period of time.

Diplomystus, or herring, from the Early Eocene

COPROLITE Fossilized animal dropping.

CORAL A build-up of polyps' skeletons, that may grow into a reef.

CRETACEOUS The last geological period of the Mesozoic, that lasted from 142 to 65 mya.

CREVASSE A deep crack in a glacier.

CRINOID Primitive echinoderm with a cupped body and branching arms.

CRUST The thin outer layer of the Earth. It varies in thickness between 7 and 70 km (4.33 and 43.5 miles) thick.

CRUSTACEAN An arthropod with a hard shell, jointed legs, and compound eyes.

DENDRITE A crystal that forms branches.

DEVONIAN The geological period that lasted from 417 to 354 mya.

Eocene angiosperm

ECHINODERM A marine animal with five-point symmetry, for example, a starfish.

ELEMENT Material that cannot be broken down into more simple substances by chemical means.

EOCENE The geological epoch that lasted from 55 to 34 mya, when mammals became the dominant land vertebrates.

EROSION The wearing away of rock by wind, water, and ice.

EVOLUTION The process by which species change into new ones over millions of generations. It happens as some characteristics are kept and others are lost.

EXOSKELETON Tough outer casing that protects the body of some invertebrates.

EXTINCT Describes an animal or plant that has died out.

FOSSIL The naturally-preserved remains of animals or plants, or evidence of them.

FOSSIL FUEL Materials formed from the remains of ancient living things, that can be burned to give off energy, for example, oil.

GEOLOGY The study of rocks.

GLACIER A slow-moving river of ice.

GYMNOSPERM A plant that produces and protects its seeds in a cone.

HERBIVORE Grazing or browsing animal.

HOLOCENE Our present geological epoch, which began 10,000 years ago, when humans became the dominant land vertebrates.

HOMINID A member of the family *Hominidae*, which includes extinct and modern humans.

ICTHYOSAUR An extinct, dolphin-like marine reptile that lived in the Mesozoic.

IGNEOUS ROCK Rock formed as magma cooled and hardened in the Earth's crust.

IMPERVIOUS Describes rock that liquid cannot penetrate.

INVERTEBRATE An animal without a backbone, for example, a shellfish or insect.

JURASSIC The geological period that lasted from 206 to 142 mya.

LIMESTONE A sedimentary rock made of the fossilized remains of ancient creatures.

LYCOPOD The clubmosses, a group of primitive plants that reproduce by spores.

MAGMA Molten rock beneath the Earth's surface.

MAMMAL A warm-blooded, hair-covered animal that usually gives birth to live young.

MESOZOIC The geological era that lasted from 248 to 65 mya, also known as the age of the dinosaurs.

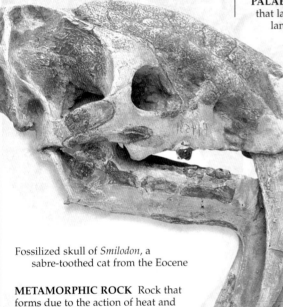

Fossilized skull of *Smilodon*, a sabre-toothed cat from the Eocene

METAMORPHIC ROCK Rock that forms due to the action of heat and pressure, or heat alone.

MINERAL A solid mixture of chemicals that has certain regular characteristics, such as atomic structure. The name relates to mining.

MIOCENE The geological epoch that lasted from 24 to five mya.

MOLLUSC An invertebrate that is unsegmented.

NATURALIST Someone who studies nature, especially animals or plants.

NODULE A rounded lump of hard rock.

OLIGOCENE The geological epoch that lasted from 34 to 24 mya.

OPAL A gem composed of hydrous silica.

ORDOVICIAN The geological period that lasted from 495 to 443 mya.

ORE Rock from which metal is extracted.

PALAEOBOTANY The study of fossilized plants.

PALAEOCENE The first geological epoch of the Cenozoic. It lasted from 65 to 55 mya.

PALAEONTOLOGY The study of fossils.

PALAEOZOIC The geological era that lasted from 545 to 248 mya, when land plants developed and the dominant animals were fish and marine invertebrates.

PANGAEA Supercontinent that formed in the Late Palaeozoic and began to break up in the Mesozoic.

PERMIAN The last geological period of the Palaeozoic. It lasted from 290 to 248 mya.

PIGMENT The chemicals that give something its colouring.

PLACODERM An extinct fish with armour and jaws that lived from the Late Silurian to the Early Carboniferous.

PLEISTOCENE The geological epoch that lasted from two million to 10,000 ya, the time of the last Ice Age.

PLESIOSAUR An extinct, long-necked marine reptile that lived in the Mesozoic.

PLIOCENE The geological epoch that lasted from five to two mya.

POLYP A tiny marine invertebrate. Whole colonies of polyps form corals and reefs.

PRECAMBRIAN The earliest geological period, which lasted from 4,600 mya, when Earth formed, until 545 mya.

PTEROSAUR An extinct flying reptile that lived in the Mesozoic.

REPTILE A cold-blooded, scaly animal that usually reproduces by laying eggs.

RESOURCE A useful material. Natural resources include wood, oil, and iron.

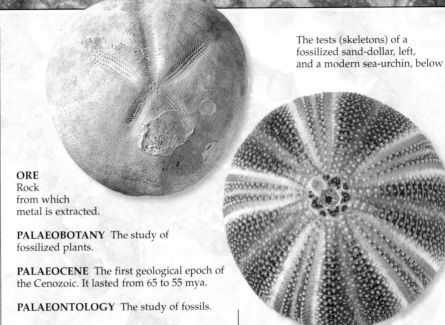

The tests (skeletons) of a fossilized sand-dollar, left, and a modern sea-urchin, below

ROCK Solid mixtures, or aggregates, of minerals.

SEDIMENTARY ROCK Rock that forms at the Earth's surface. It is made of layers of rock fragments and other substances such as mud that have been deposited on top of each other.

SHALE A rock made of compacted clay.

SILURIAN The geological period that lasted from 443 to 417 mya.

STRATIFICATION The formation of layers, or bands, of rock.

TEST An echinoid's plated skeleton.

TRACE FOSSIL Fossilized evidence of the activities of an animal, such as burrows, footprints, or coprolites.

TRIASSIC The first geological period of the Mesozoic. It lasted from 248 to 248 mya.

VERTEBRATE An animal with a backbone, such as a fish, frog, or human being.

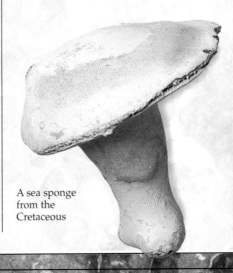

A sea sponge from the Cretaceous

Index

Acknowledgements

Dorling Kindersley would like to thank:
Plymouth Marine Laboratory, National Museum of Wales, Kew Gardens for specimens for photography; Lester Cheeseman and Thomas Keenes for additional design assistance; Anna Kunst for editorial assistance; Meryl Silbert; Karl Shone for additional photography (pp. 18–19); Jane Parker for the index

The author would like to thank:
M.K. Howarth; C Patterson; R.A. Fortey; C.H.C. Brunton; A.W. Gentry; B.R. Rosen; J.B. Richardson; P.L. Forey; N.J. Morris; C.B. Stringer; A.B. Smith; J.E.P. Whittaker; R. Croucher; S.F. Morris; C.R. Hill; A.C. Milner; R.L. Hodgkinson; C.A. Walker; R.J. Cleevely; C.H. Shute; V.T. Young; D.N. Lewis; A.E. Longbottom; M. Crawley; R. Kruszynski; C. Bell; S.C. Naylor; A. Lum; R.W. Ingle; P.D. Jenkins; P.D. Hillyard; D.T. Moore; J.W. Schopf; C.M. Butler; P.W. Jackson

Picture Credits
t=top, b=bottom, m=middle, l=left, r=right

Aldus Archive: 53tm, 54bl;
Alison Anholt-White: 28tl;
Ardea: 9bl, 21m, 42m, 42bl, 43t, 61tm;
Biofotos/Heather Angel: 26m, 31mr, 39br, 44–5bm, 60tr;
Booth Museum of Natural History 66bl;
Bridgeman Art Library: 14mr; /Musée Cluny/Lauros-Giraudon 17tl;
Dept. of Earth Sciences, University of Cambridge: 39mr;
Cleveland Museum of Natural History, Ohio: 59m;
Bruce Coleman: 8br, 22m; /Jeff Foote 28tr, 39m, 40m; /Fritz Prenzel 57br; /Kim Campbell 59ml;
Simon Conway Morris: 20m;

Corbis: James L. Amos 65br, 68bl;
Mary Evans Picture Library: 13ml, 14br, 15tl, 20m, 48t, 52tl, 54t, 54br, 55t, 55mr, 55b, 62m;
Vivien Fifield: 50bl;
Geological Society: 46t;
Geoscience Features Picture Library: 9tr, 51tl, 51tm, 51tr;
David George: 25m;
Robert Harding Picture Library: 21br, 29m, 59b;
Michael Holford: 12tl;
Hunterian Museum: 66tl;
Hutchison Library: 24tl, 57mr;
Mansell Collection: 26t, 40b;
Natural History Museum, London: 66tr, 70m, 66tm, 66ml, 66bm (below), 69t; /Geological Museum of China 64tl;
Oxford Scientific Films: 44bl, 53bm;
Oxford University Museum: 66br (above), 71tm, 71b;

Planet Earth Pictures: 32ml, 41m, 43ml, 44mr, 63tl;
Rex Features: Sipa Press 65m;
Ann Ronan Picture Library: 15tm, 50br;
Royal Tyrell Museum, Canada: 66bm (above);
Science Photo Library: 58r; /Tony Craddock 65bl; /Peter Menzel 64b; /Philippe Plailly 68t; /Philippe Plailly/Eurelios 69ml, 69mr; /Andrew Syred 67mr (above)
Paul Taylor: 19b;
University Museum of Zoology, Cambridge: 69b; /Sarah Finney (GLAHM 100815) 65t;
ZEFA: 20–21bl

Illustrations by: John Woodcock, Eugene Fleury
Original picture research by: Kathy Lockley